> *She knew how to swing her legs on that hyphen that defined and denied who she was: Iranian-American. Neither the first word nor the second really belonged to her. Her place was on the hyphen, and on the hyphen she would stay, carrying memories of the one place from which she had come and the other place in which she must succeed.*
>
> —MARJAN KAMALI, AUTHOR OF *TOGETHER TEA*, *THE STATIONERY SHOP*, AND *THE LION WOMEN OF TEHRAN*

BITTER & SWEET

GLOBAL FLAVORS FROM AN IRANIAN-AMERICAN KITCHEN

OMID ROUSTAEI

weldon**owen**

TO RICHARD,
who opened my eyes and rekindled my
connection with Iran in ways previously unimagined.
Without your unwavering support, this book
would have remained a mere dream.

CONTENTS

FOREWORD 8

INTRODUCTION 11

THE ART OF COOKING 14

THE INGREDIENTS 16

CHAPTER 1
SALADS AND STARTERS 19
A Carefree Childhood
Tehran and Daryakenar, Iran | Pre-1979

CHAPTER 2
SOUPS AND ĀSHES 39
The Pointed Gun
Tehran, Iran | 1979–1983

CHAPTER 3
KUKUS 57
The Immigrant Life
Sedona, AZ | 1984

CHAPTER 4
VEGETABLE DISHES 69
An American Identity
Seattle, WA | 1993

CHAPTER 5
RICE DISHES 89
The Open Door
Boulder, CO | 1998

CHAPTER 6
KHORESHES 125
Embracing the Apron
Seattle, WA | 1998

CHAPTER 7
KABABS, BURGERS, AND FISH 165
The Therapist Within
Seattle, WA | 2001

CHAPTER 8
BREADS 183
Reconnection
San Jose, CA, and Seattle, WA | 2014–2017

CHAPTER 9
DESSERTS 199
The Caspian Chef
Seattle, WA | 2017

CHAPTER 10
BEVERAGES 217
The Weight of Hope
Milnathort, Scotland, and Seattle, WA | 2022

EPILOGUE 229
American Cuisine

ACKNOWLEDGMENTS 234

ABOUT THE AUTHOR 235

INDEX 236

FOREWORD

To anyone else whose existence also dances on the proverbial hyphen—the core of who you are composed of many disparate influences—this comprehensive sensory adventure will feel like a homecoming. Like sitting down to tea with a kindred spirit, drinking in *Bitter & Sweet* is to be seen and nourished just as you are.

My own heritage stems from a father who immigrated to the United States from Hong Kong and a mother whose family is part of the Chinese diaspora in Latin America. I myself was born and raised in California, bouncing back and forth between sunny San Diego and my grandparents' house in Tegucigalpa, and eventually growing into an adult life that sent me around the world before landing in the greenery of the Pacific Northwest.

Occupying an amalgam of Chinese-Honduran-American cultures and having set roots in many different places, I understand the bittersweetness of always feeling both home and homesick. This beautiful cookbook is a pure encapsulation of this.

Candidly, prior to meeting Omid, my personal connection to Iranian cuisine didn't extend much beyond an appreciation of saffron-scented crispy tahdig. I know, it's terribly cliché of me. I've since had the privilege of attending one of his cooking classes and have replicated a number of his recipes in my own home kitchen. In spite of my limited expertise, I still feel deeply connected to this book and Omid's unique brand of Iranian-inspired fare clearly shaped by his lived experiences.

Bitter & Sweet is a fully engaging journey. Generously filled with detailed recipes complete with time-saving suggestions and accessible substitutions, this book also provides essential tips for cooking intuitively. Dishes like khoresh hulu, a wonderfully fragrant peach and saffron chicken stew, and ash jo, a hearty barley and bean soup, have become instant favorites in my household. To say nothing of the za'atar herb sauce I've adapted to what I have in the fridge at any given moment and which I slather over everything.

But more than sharing comfort foods that are sure to appeal broadly, Omid also shares intimately from his childhood experiences, divulges his stories of subsequent transformation and self-reinvention, and notably sheds any veneer of fairy-tale narratives. His vulnerability is paramount. The recipes in this cookbook are rich with flavor and meaning, the stories vibrant and complex, and by melding everything together, Omid offers us all a way home.

This book inspired me in myriad ways, and I know it will do the same for you. What Omid has created here is a gift of exploration and discovery.

Here's to finding and being found. And feasting on the most delicious Iranian and global food along the way.

—LAUREN KO, BESTSELLING AUTHOR OF
PIEOMETRY AND FOUNDER OF @LOKOKITCHEN

INTRODUCTION

It's been forty years since I moved from Iran to the United States as a teenager. Forty years of adaptation, integration, learning, loss, gain, discarding my origins, and finding them again. Forty years of becoming the person I am today: an Iranian-American.

Even before it became my profession, food was a constant in my life. Food defined the daily schedule of my childhood in Iran. As a newly arrived immigrant in the United States, I enthusiastically adopted typical American foods as a way of fitting in. As a young professional in the biotech industry, I relieved my work stress by indulging in PBS cooking shows and cooking classes. And for well over twenty years now, I've been sharing my passion for food with others: as a personal chef; as a culinary instructor; as a food writer, photographer, and videographer; as a recipe developer; and as an advocate for Iranian cuisine (not to mention as the primary cook in a very foodie family).

This book is a natural next step for me, but it took me a long time to determine what exactly I wanted to say. I knew that I didn't want to produce a picture-perfect volume of cheerful stories and scenes featuring a joyful child perched on a kitchen counter, dusted with flour, absorbing family traditions from a smiling grandparent. I'm also not the right person to create a comprehensive book of historical research on Iranian cuisine, presenting dishes in their most authentic, traditional form.

With my best friends in Daryakenar, Iran, around 1975. We had no idea how our bond would be disrupted by unforeseen forces.

Perhaps unsurprisingly, what emerged is largely a reflection of the way I teach Iranian food and traditions in my cooking classes. I want to provide more than a set of rigid instructions and cultural facts. Rather, I want to inspire curiosity, tell stories, teach you how I approach cooking, and encourage you to experiment, not only with Iranian ingredients and techniques but also with the range of cuisines that I've been fortunate enough to explore during my culinary career. This is the most genuine and authentic book I could produce. I hope it will make you feel as though I'm standing beside you, guiding you thoughtfully through each step.

Most of the recipes in this book showcase Iranian dishes, some well known and some less familiar, and often with my personal twists. As I teach and demonstrate the techniques and nuances of this cuisine, I often encounter students who are unfamiliar with it or are intimidated by its perceived complexity. My mission has always been to make Iranian cuisine more inviting and accessible to my non-Iranian students.

I intentionally refrain from labeling any dish as strictly "authentic" or "traditional." The food I grew up with in Iran was undoubtedly authentic, but leaving as a teenager and learning to cook from the books available to me in the United States led to new interpretations. Additionally, living far from Iran meant that my access to certain ingredients was limited, further challenging the concept of authenticity. Therefore, I fully embrace flexibility and improvisation in cooking, skills honed through years of self-teaching, culinary education, and exploration.

I often compare Iranian cooking to weaving a Persian rug: both involve a rich tapestry of colors, textures, balance, design, patience, and, above all, love. Iranian cuisine is a symphony of flavors and aromas, rarely spicy, instead characterized by a delicate interplay of sour and sweet elements. Sourness often takes the lead, with bitterness, sweetness, and salt as supporting notes.

Food is an integral part of Iranian culture, with meals served family style. Expect generous portions of light, fluffy basmati rice, prized for its crispy layer, known as tahdig, at the bottom. The rice is accompanied by vegetables, herbs, or meticulously simmered stews. Saffron, tomatoes, and herbs in abundance form the foundation of Iranian stews, providing a canvas to showcase various meats and vegetables.

In addition to the Iranian-inspired dishes you'll find here, I've included some highlights from my exploration of other cuisines and cooking styles. These range from products of my formal training in plant-based, improvisational cooking to favorites I've accumulated during my travels.

All of these recipes, be they Iranian rice dishes or stews, braised tofu, or Scottish smoked fish soup, connect me to my heritage and to my identity today. My aim is to take you on a journey of flavors and stories, to share knowledge and spark curiosity about how humanity grapples with disconnection and strives for belonging.

This is, of course, at its heart a cookbook. But writing it has also been a deeply personal journey of self-discovery. In the hope of shedding more light on the Iranian-American experience, I have interspersed each section of recipes with short chapters about my own story. These are not all lighthearted anecdotes or happy experiences, though I hope they properly reflect my appreciation for the many opportunities and privileges that have come my way. Overall, I have tried to be honest and thoughtful.

Mine is not a story of destiny, but one of unexpected circumstances that shaped my identity through my connection with food. Instead of dwelling on what could have been, my story now revolves around resilience and determination to build human connections through the transformative art of food and cooking.

THE ART OF COOKING

IMPROVISATION AND INTUITION

At first glance, including a chapter on improvisation and intuition in a recipe book might seem, well, counterintuitive. After all, recipes typically contain precise instructions that you might feel compelled to follow carefully. However, I've come to understand that sticking closely to a recipe doesn't guarantee a perfect outcome. There's an art to cooking, and I firmly believe that viewing recipes as flexible guidelines rather than rigid rules is essential.

My approach to food started to be shaped as I used multiple sources to teach myself to prepare Iranian cuisine. The flexibility I gained during that process was then reinforced in my culinary education, which emphasized the importance of improvisational and intuitive cooking.

There are several reasons why deviating from a recipe can be beneficial. Sometimes, certain ingredients may be unavailable or hard to find, or perhaps you want to cater to your own preferences or dietary needs. In such situations, improvisation becomes crucial as you explore and learn to skillfully substitute ingredients.

Also, cooking inherently involves variability: in freshness and intensity of ingredients, in stove temperatures, in kitchen equipment, and in skills and approaches of the cook, to name just a few factors. These can all materially impact the outcome of a dish. Therefore, I encourage you to liberate yourself from the strict confines of recipe instructions and use your intuition, letting your senses take the lead.

Flexibility is not simply an appropriate response to availability of ingredients and variability in the cooking process. It is also an opportunity. I relish the experience of surveying my pantry and fridge and crafting a meal with the ingredients at hand, rather than starting with a long grocery list and a shopping trip. In some ways, it's like paying homage to how previous generations used to prepare their meals.

Throughout this book, I've suggested substitutions when you find yourself missing an ingredient. You can still create a delicious outcome using another protein, vegetable, or herb. Don't confine yourself to my suggestions, though. There's nothing I'd like better than to know that a recipe in this book was the starting point for a dish you created that I never even contemplated.

Intuitive cooking involves delving into the depths of our senses, offering profound knowledge from within that can be used to guide our decisions in the kitchen. Engaging our sight, smell, touch, hearing, taste, and emotions is a skill that can be developed and nurtured through practice and dedication.

From the nerve endings in my fingertips to the taste buds on my tongue, from my interpretation of cooking sounds to my strong sense of smell for rich spices and my visual adoration of fragrant herbs, all these senses intertwine, forming a direct connection to my central nervous system and emotional core. Each sensory input evokes a unique set of emotions and responses, thereby influencing my culinary decisions.

Imagine picking up a bottle of strong distilled vinegar. How would you react upon visually examining it? And when you open it and smell it? How different would that experience be with, say, a bottle of rose water, cayenne pepper, or ground cinnamon? Try this at home, and you'll quickly notice that your instinctive reactions reveal valuable information. Some ingredients might pull you in with a smile; others might lead you to push them away with concern or distaste.

Aromas, in particular, offer invaluable insights into the potency of ingredients and their potential impact on a dish. In intuitive cooking, the sense of smell becomes a powerful guide, helping us understand the potential effect of each ingredient on the final outcome. Our instinctive reactions to different scents shape our culinary decisions and influence the overall taste of our creations.

To determine the appropriate amount of an ingredient, I use my senses of touch and sight rather than relying on precise measurements. For example, I pick up coarse sea salt with my fingers and crush dried herbs in the palm of my hand before adding them to any dish. Sounds, such as sautéing vegetables or simmering stews, provide essential cues about the cooking process. And arguably the most crucial aspect is that I taste the dish repeatedly from start to finish.

To assist you on this journey, I've included as many sensory cues as possible in the recipes. When you try them out, I encourage you to approach them as opportunities for exploration and creativity. Embrace the art of intuitive cooking, and let your senses guide you in crafting delightful and personalized dishes.

THE INGREDIENTS

Setting up a pantry to help you venture into Iranian-inspired cooking may initially appear a bit daunting. But augmenting what's already in your kitchen with a relatively small number of new items, and using substitutes where necessary, will allow you to prepare the dishes in this book.

This section includes a few ingredients that I think of as essentials in Iranian cuisine. Don't be discouraged if you want to try a recipe before you've added a specific item to your pantry. Many have good substitutes, which I've included extensively in the recipes. Give the alternatives a try, and then pick up the specific ingredient the next time you have the chance. Many of them are available in the "international" or "ethnic" aisle of your nearby supermarket, and the more obscure items can be located at a local Iranian or West Asian market or ordered online.

Between new ingredients and appropriate substitutes, I hope to give you the foundation to be creative and improvise as you venture out into the world of Iranian cuisine.

Āb ghureh (verjuice or verjus) is produced by harvesting and juicing grapes before they ripen. It's used as a souring agent in soups and stews. In mid-spring, unripe grapes can be purchased and stored in the freezer.

Barberries are exceptionally tart dried red berries that offer a uniquely sharp flavor, particularly in rice and kuku (Iranian-style frittata) dishes. When combined with saffron, sugar, and butter, they also become a standard topping for numerous dishes.

Fenugreek leaves are grown and used all around the world, but are embraced particularly by Iranians, Indians, and Pakistanis. Fenugreek emits a potent yet pleasantly sweet aroma. When added to rice dishes or stews in the right quantities, it imparts a unique depth and flavor, but be careful not to use too much, which can result in an undesirable harshness. There are no really good substitutes for fenugreek, but celery leaves have some similarities.

Golpar (Persian hogweed) is a flowering plant native to Iran, with small pods that are intensely aromatic with a slightly bitter, citrusy taste. Ground to a fine powder, golpar is used as a topping for stews, spreads, and cooked beans. It also adds an enticingly contrasting element when sprinkled on fresh watermelon and pomegranates!

Kashk (fermented whey) is a thick, sour sauce made from yogurt that's available in sealed jars. It's used either as a main component of soups and stews or as a topping for them, and in either case it adds a rich and salty umami kick, a little like sour cream but much more robust.

Limu omāni (Persian dried limes) are small limes that are simmered in brine before being left out to dry in the sun. This lengthy process creates a somewhat intimidating

dark, wrinkled skin, but it also gives the limes an unmatched flavor that is intensely citrusy and tart yet musky and earthy. Limu omāni are pierced with a knife or sliced in half before being added to stews for a highly distinctive sourness.

Pomegranate paste/molasses is a highly concentrated paste made by simmering and reducing fresh pomegranate juice. Used in soups, stews, and spreads, it adds a rich maroon color and a unique blend of tart and sweet flavors. In my experience, no two bottles of pomegranate molasses taste alike, and their sweet-tart balance can be unpredictable. Before settling on your favorite brand, examine the label for added sugar or other ingredients. Ideally, choose a brand that lists pomegranates as the sole ingredient.

Rose water and orange blossom water are potent floral essences used throughout Iranian cuisine in both sweet and savory dishes. They are frequently used in baking—a little like vanilla and other extracts in Western culinary traditions—and to add playful floral aromas to stews.

Saffron, the crown jewel of Iranian cuisine, refers to the deep red threads of the crocus flower. It imparts a bright, golden-yellow color; a sweet, floral scent; and a rich, earthy flavor. Saffron threads are typically ground into a fine powder and bloomed in a small amount of hot water. This is added toward the end of the cooking process to preserve its aroma and color. Saffron is best stored in an airtight container in a dark, cool location; I keep mine in the fridge.

Sumac, the ground-up dried berries from the sumac shrub, has a deep burgundy hue and a tangy, lemony taste. It's a versatile addition to a variety of dishes, from kababs and salads to soups and dressings. Sprinkled atop rice, sumac's unique flavor adds depth and brightens the taste profile.

Tamarind paste, most commonly found in dishes from the southern region of Iran, is an intensely tart product made from the pods of the tamarind tree. Diluted with water, it's used in rice, stews, and soups, adding a distinct and potent sour taste.

CHAPTER 1

SALADS AND STARTERS

Lettuce Cups with Cucumbers
and Yogurt Sumac Dressing • **V GF**
22

Citrus and Beet Salad with Fennel Dressing • **V GF**
The Pantry's Iranian-American Salad • 25

Beet Salad with Tarragon Dressing • **VG GF**
27

Pomegranate and Cucumber Salad • **V GF**
Sālād Anār-o Khiār • 29

Minty Cucumber and Tomato Salad • **VG GF**
Sālād Shirāzi • 30

Kale and Crispy Chickpea Salad • **V GF**
31

Feta Pesto on a Crispy Baguette • **V**
Iranian Bruschetta • 32

Fried Potato and Bulgur Kibbeh
Kibbet Batata bil Lahmeh • 35

V • VEGETARIAN   **VG** • VEGAN   **GF** • GLUTEN FREE

A CAREFREE CHILDHOOD

TEHRAN AND DARYAKENAR, IRAN | PRE-1979

Rice dishes, whether simple or elaborate and saffron-infused. Aromatic, colorful, and complex stews. Delicate traditional pastries and desserts. All of these remind me of who I am and where I come from.

The flavors of Iran permeated my early years, to an extent that I didn't really understand until much later in life. The aromas of vibrant herbs and intoxicating spices, and the sounds of sautéing onions and simmering stews, were the backdrop to my childhood. Now I see clearly how food was so much more than just sustenance: It was a component of my sense of stability and security, a symbol of continuity and connection, a taste of my heritage. Eating Iranian style meant abundance, sharing, and generous hospitality governed by tārof, a tradition of elaborate rituals by both host and guest.

Food was a source of consistency and predictability in our household, dictated by gender roles and division of labor. My father took responsibility for shopping and gathering ingredients, while my mother prepared the meals. As a child, I would hover in the kitchen, hoping to snatch some cooked chicken or fried potatoes before they were added to the meal. Now I wonder whether my mother took her son's mischievousness into consideration when planning the dishes.

Food guided our daily schedule, which revolved around when meals were served. We almost always ate family style in the kitchen, often sharing meals with extended family and other guests. Infrequently, as a treat, I would be permitted to eat my food in front of the TV, watching Friday morning cartoons (Friday is the primary weekend day in Iran).

While we lived in Tehran, both of my parents had strong preferences for the traditional dishes of the Caspian Sea region, where they had grown up. I, too, had distinct preferences; though I never considered myself a picky eater, there were certain foods I welcomed on my plate and others I skillfully managed to avoid.

Tomatoes, celery, spinach, zucchini, and eggplant topped my list of dislikes. Whenever we ate hamburgers, I would slyly pass my tomatoes to my dad, who loved them. Cooked tomatoes were slightly more tolerable; fortunately so, since at least half of traditional Persian dishes contain tomatoes or tomato products.

When it came to celery, particularly in dishes like khoresh karafs (celery stew), I assiduously avoided serving myself this unpleasantly strange-tasting vegetable. Instead, I loaded up on beef or chicken pieces, while strategically ensuring that the quantity of meat didn't earn disapproving glances from family members.

Spinach was a lost cause, with its finely chopped leaves blended seamlessly into dishes, leaving no room for escape. As for zucchini, I could tolerate it, but I still wanted my protests to be acknowledged.

Eggplant was an absolute no-no in any form, and I refused to yield to pressure to consume it. My persistent opposition eventually paid off, and my parents became more flexible with their culinary rules. Occasionally, I was even allowed to raid the freezer, thaw some hot dogs, and substitute them for eggplant in an Iranian-style omelet. To this day, I associate eggplant with hot dogs and a feeling of triumph!

The Caspian Sea, known as Darya Khazar in Iran, was another influence that shaped my childhood. Since my parents came from the beautiful city of Babol, we frequently embarked on trips from Tehran to visit our family there. Eventually, we acquired a villa in a suburb called Daryakenar, right on the shores of the Caspian Sea. Our visits became increasingly frequent, often accompanied by large groups of friends and family members. I spent my summers building sandcastles, flying kites on the beach, and embarking on countless adventures on my high-handlebar banana-seat bike.

The route from Tehran to Daryakenar first crosses the Alborz Mountains, passing Iran's highest peak, Mount Damavand, before dropping down into the coastal plain. My mother always prepared picnic food for the long drive, but we would also stop at roadside stalls to buy kababs and—as we approached the sea—balāl (sweet corn), grilled and then plunged into salt water.

Family meals in Daryakenar were adapted to feature the outstanding local produce: I still remember the fresh squash, incredibly flavorful eggs, and abundance of herbs. In otherwise familiar stews, duck would often replace chicken. And on special occasions my mother would prepare a showstopping dish of duck stuffed with vegetables, nuts, and dried fruits and glazed with pomegranate molasses.

> *When you are displaced from a place against your will, your appreciation for the way that place shaped you and the role it played in your life is magnified.*
>
> —DR. CLINT SMITH

Just thinking of this quaint suburb still evokes an intense sense of homesickness and nostalgia. It's not so much the visuals that flood my mind, but rather the scents and the climate that define this place. I can still recall the fragrance of the rice paddies and the sensation of the moist, humid air against my skin.

I have had to say good-bye to the Caspian Sea twice now: once shortly before I left Iran, and a second time when the house in Daryakenar was finally sold to finance my education in the United States. To this day, I long to immerse myself in that water again and savor its touch and taste. The yearning to reunite with the sea persists, an unfulfilled desire.

LETTUCE CUPS WITH CUCUMBERS AND YOGURT SUMAC DRESSING

MAKES 6 SERVINGS • **V GF**

For me, the star of this salad is the yogurt sumac dressing, taking the crunchy vegetables nestled inside lettuce cups to a whole new level.

- ½ cup (120 ml) whole milk Greek yogurt
- 2 tablespoons red wine vinegar
- 1 small shallot, finely minced
- 2 cloves garlic, minced
- 1 teaspoon sea salt
- ½ teaspoon ground black pepper
- 1 tablespoon dried mint
- 1 tablespoon ground sumac
- 8 Persian cucumbers (about 1¼ lb/570 g total), thinly sliced
- 4 radishes, thinly sliced
- 1 head Bibb lettuce, cut into 6 wedges
- 2 tablespoons olive oil
- ¼ cup (30 g) walnuts, coarsely chopped

Blend the yogurt, vinegar, shallot, garlic, salt, pepper, mint, and sumac in a medium mixing bowl to make the dressing.

Add the sliced cucumbers and radishes and mix until they are nicely coated.

Take the Bibb lettuce wedges and arrange them like little cups on a serving platter. Scoop the yogurt-dressed cucumber and radish mixture into the lettuce cups, drizzle with the olive oil, and sprinkle the chopped walnuts on top of the salad.

> **NOTES**
>
> *Napa or red cabbage leaves make excellent substitutions for Bibb lettuce. You can also replace the vinegar with lemon or lime juice, along with the zest, to add extra flavor to the dressing.*

The Pantry's Iranian-American Salad

CITRUS AND BEET SALAD WITH FENNEL DRESSING

MAKES 4 SERVINGS • V GF

The Pantry in Seattle is a gathering place that unites people through food, classes, and shared meals with an emphasis on storytelling and social justice. I've been part of The Pantry family since 2019, and it's where I've focused my teaching efforts in recent years.

In January 2023, I hosted two special dinners at The Pantry to bring attention to the Woman, Life, Freedom movement in Iran. At each event, my colleagues and I served an Iranian feast to forty guests from diverse backgrounds. Our aim was to unite people, raise awareness, and highlight the ongoing events in Iran. Alongside traditional dishes, we created this salad to blend Iranian and American ingredients and flavors.

FOR THE PICKLED BEETS

1 large red beet, peeled and cut into irregular bite-size pieces

1½ cups (360 ml) water

½ teaspoon sea salt

½ cup (100 g) unrefined cane sugar

½ cup (120 ml) distilled white vinegar

2 tablespoons olive oil

1 tablespoon pickling spice

1 teaspoon red pepper flakes

Honey (optional)

To make the pickled beets, place all of the ingredients in a small saucepan and bring to a gentle simmer. Cover and cook over low heat until the beets can be easily pierced with a knife, 30–40 minutes. Remove from the heat and let the beets cool in the pickling liquid. Once cooled, strain the beets through a colander, transfer to a small bowl, and set them aside. Discard the pickling liquid.

CONTINUED

SALADS AND STARTERS

FOR THE DRESSING

½ head fennel, cored and cut into small pieces

2 cloves garlic

2 tablespoons white wine vinegar

2 tablespoons finely chopped fresh mint

2 teaspoons dried mint

2 teaspoons honey

½ teaspoon sea salt

½ teaspoon ground black pepper

¼ cup (60 ml) olive oil

¼ cup (60 ml) safflower oil

FOR THE SALAD

1 orange, preferably Cara Cara or navel

1 blood orange

4 Persian cucumbers, sliced diagonally

2 on-the-vine tomatoes, quartered and seeded

½ cup (15 g) coarsely chopped fresh parsley

1 shallot, finely minced

To make the dressing, combine the fennel, garlic, white wine vinegar, fresh and dried mint, honey, salt, and pepper in a high-powered blender. Blend until coarsely mixed.

With the blender running at high speed, drizzle in the oils to create an emulsified dressing. Taste and adjust the seasoning with more salt and honey if necessary. Set aside.

To make the salad, cut off the ends of the oranges and, using a paring knife, supreme them by removing the peel and pith. Slice into the sections between the membranes and remove the seeds. Place the orange segments in a small bowl along with their juice.

In a mixing bowl, combine the cucumbers, tomatoes, parsley, and shallot. Add the pickled beets and enough of the mint-fennel dressing to lightly coat all of the vegetables, ⅓–½ cup (80–120 ml). Stir gently.

Arrange the mixture on a large serving platter, place the orange segments on top, and drizzle with the remaining orange juice.

NOTES

This recipe yields about 1 cup (240 ml) of dressing, providing extra for other salads. Store in a sealed container in the fridge for up to a week.

BEET SALAD WITH TARRAGON DRESSING

MAKES 4 SERVINGS • VG GF

This salad celebrates my unwavering love for the vibrant beet and my years of teaching plant-based cooking classes, where I emphasized improvisation. Though I experimented with many ingredients, I consistently showcased a beet salad and converted many non-beet enthusiasts into fans!

4 beets (about 1¼ lb/ 570 g total), scrubbed

1½ teaspoons sea salt, divided

¼ cup (60 ml) olive oil

¼ cup (60 ml) aged balsamic vinegar

1 small shallot, minced

2 cloves garlic, minced

1 tablespoon chopped fresh tarragon

¼ teaspoon ground black pepper

2 green onions, thinly sliced

2 tablespoons roasted pepitas

Trim the roots and stems of the beets and place them in a large saucepan. Cover with water, add 1 teaspoon of the salt, and bring it to a boil. Once boiling, reduce the heat to a simmer, cover, and let the beets cook until they are tender, about 45 minutes. You can check their readiness by inserting a paring knife into the beets—if it goes in smoothly, they're good to go!

While the beets are cooking, we can prepare the dressing. Grab a large mixing bowl and whisk together the oil, vinegar, shallot, garlic, tarragon, pepper, and remaining ½ teaspoon of salt. Set aside.

Once the beets have cooked, we need to cool them down quickly. Prepare a large bowl of ice water and, using a slotted spoon, remove the beets from the pan and immerse them in the ice water. Discard the cooking liquid. Now, peel the beets and slice them into ¼-inch (6-mm)-thick slices.

Add the sliced beets and the green onions to the mixing bowl with the dressing. If you have them on hand, chop a couple of beet stems and leaves and add them as well. Give everything a good toss and place it in the fridge to marinate for at least an hour.

Transfer the beets to a serving platter and top with the roasted pepitas.

> **NOTES**
> *If you buy your beets with stems and leaves attached, add a few to the salad for some extra color and crunch.*

Sālād Anār-o Khiār

POMEGRANATE AND CUCUMBER SALAD

MAKES 4 SERVINGS • V GF

Pomegranates take center stage in the dinner spread celebrating the winter solstice, *shab-e yaldā* in Persian. This salad is a personal favorite of mine for this holiday.

FOR THE DRESSING

¼ cup (60 ml) olive oil

¼ cup (60 ml) red wine vinegar

1 teaspoon sea salt

½ teaspoon ground black pepper

¼ teaspoon ground golpar (Persian hogweed)

FOR THE SALAD

6 Persian cucumbers or 1 English cucumber (about 1 lb/450 g total), thinly sliced

1 cup (175 g) pomegranate seeds, from 1–2 pomegranates

¼ small red onion, thinly sliced

½ cup (15 g) thinly sliced fresh mint

½ cup (70 g) crumbled feta cheese

To make the dressing, in a small mixing bowl, combine the ingredients and whisk them together until blended.

To make the salad, in a serving bowl, mix all of the ingredients except the feta cheese. Drizzle the dressing over the salad just before serving, and sprinkle the feta cheese on top.

NOTES

Golpar, Persian hogweed, is a small, thin seedpod that adds a highly aromatic, pungent, and slightly bitter touch, and a small amount goes a long way. There really is no good substitute for golpar, but you can leave it out altogether or use some minced garlic to replace at least some of its complexity.

Sālād Shirāzi

MINTY CUCUMBER AND TOMATO SALAD

MAKES 4 SERVINGS · **VG GF**

Whether you're dining casually at home, at a formal dinner, or in a restaurant, sālād shirāzi is a common sight in Iran. Its simplicity and refreshing taste complement any meal.

FOR THE SALAD

6 Persian cucumbers or 1 English cucumber (about 1 lb/450 g total), finely diced

2 tomatoes, finely diced

½ small red onion, finely diced

FOR THE DRESSING

¼ cup (60 ml) āb ghureh (unripe grape juice)

¼ cup (60 ml) olive oil

1 tablespoon dried mint

½ teaspoon sea salt

½ teaspoon ground black pepper

To make the salad, toss the cucumbers, tomatoes, and onion together in a mixing bowl.

To make the dressing, combine the ingredients in a separate mixing bowl and give them a good stir.

Pour the dressing over the vegetables, toss, and serve.

> **NOTES**
>
> *You can find āb ghureh, unripe grape juice, in Iranian markets; otherwise, freshly squeezed lime juice is a great alternative.*
>
> *You can also add veggies like radishes, peppers, and leafy greens to customize the salad according to your liking.*
>
> *For optimal freshness and crispness, it's best to serve sālād shirāzi shortly after dressing it. If you want to make it in advance, keep the vegetable mixture and the dressing separate until just before serving.*

KALE AND CRISPY CHICKPEA SALAD

MAKES 6 SERVINGS • V GF

For nearly twenty years, I shared my love of cooking by teaching an extensive plant-based curriculum at my local food co-op, introducing the art of improvisational and intuitive cooking. To prepare for these endeavors, I would arrive hours before class, diligently shop, get everything ready, and surprise my students with an improvisational meal to start the sessions. During my preparations, I would often grab a kale salad from the co-op. This is my tribute to the salad that nourished me for countless years.

FOR THE SALAD

¼ cup (30 g) pitted Kalamata olives, sliced

4 stems kale, ribs removed, thinly sliced

6 stems Swiss chard, thinly sliced

1 red bell pepper, diced

1 small fennel bulb, thinly sliced

FOR THE DRESSING

¼ cup (60 ml) olive oil

¼ cup (60 ml) fresh lemon juice

Zest of 1 lemon

1 tablespoon honey

2 teaspoons miso

1 clove garlic, minced

½ teaspoon sea salt

¼ teaspoon ground black pepper

½ cup (15 g) coarsely chopped fresh parsley

FOR THE CHICKPEAS

1 can (15 oz/425 g) chickpeas, rinsed and drained

2 tablespoons neutral oil

¼ teaspoon chipotle pepper powder

To make the salad, grab a large mixing bowl, add all your prepped ingredients, and mix.

To make the dressing, combine the ingredients in a small mixing bowl. Blend thoroughly using a whisk to create a smooth texture.

Pour the dressing over the salad and give it a good toss. Place the salad in the fridge and let it marinate for at least 1 hour to allow the flavors to meld together and soften the leafy greens.

After about 30 minutes of marination, it's time to preheat the oven to 425°F (220°C).

To prepare the chickpeas, combine the chickpeas, oil, and chipotle pepper in a mixing bowl and mix well. Spread them out on a baking sheet in a single layer. Place the baking sheet in the oven and roast the chickpeas for about 25 minutes. Taste a couple of them to check that they are cooked to your liking—they should be soft on the inside and crispy on the outside. Once they're done, remove the baking sheet from the oven and set it aside until you're ready to serve.

Give the salad one final mix before transferring it to your serving bowl. Sprinkle the roasted chickpeas on top and serve.

Iranian Bruschetta

FETA PESTO ON A CRISPY BAGUETTE

MAKES 4 SERVINGS • V

This bruschetta is a fun twist on an Iranian classic, sabzi khordan, which is an appetizer featuring a medley of herbs served with feta cheese, green onions, radishes, and walnuts, all bunched into small pieces of flatbread. In this variation, the herbs and feta are transformed into pesto and spread onto crispy baguette slices. Not only is it delicious, but it's also a wonderful way to utilize any leftover herbs.

½ cup (15 g) fresh dill

½ cup (15 g) fresh parsley

½ cup (15 g) fresh cilantro

½ cup (15 g) fresh chives

¼ cup (25 g) walnuts

¼ cup (35 g) crumbled feta cheese

¼ cup (60 ml) olive oil

1 small baguette, cut diagonally into 6–8 slices

4 radishes, thinly sliced

1 Persian cucumber, thinly sliced

Process the herbs and walnuts in a food processor until they are coarsely chopped. Add the feta and pulse the mixture two or three times until the feta has been incorporated but has not turned creamy.

Preheat the oven to 350°F. Arrange the baguette slices on a baking sheet, brush with the olive oil, and bake until lightly toasted, about 15 minutes. Once toasted, generously spread the herb and feta pesto onto the baguette slices and top them off with the radish and cucumber slices.

> **NOTES**
>
> *Think of the baguette slices as a blank canvas for experimenting with whatever herbs, nuts, and veggies you have on hand. The ingredients here are just suggestions!*

Kibbet Batata bil Lahmeh

FRIED POTATO AND BULGUR KIBBEH

MAKES ABOUT 18 KIBBEH

Kibbeh is a beloved dish enjoyed in Palestine, Lebanon, Syria, and beyond. This is an original recipe graciously shared by my dear friend and culinary colleague Nadia Tommalieh. Nadia is a well-respected culinary educator who wholeheartedly preserves and shares the rich flavors and traditions of her Palestinian heritage.

FOR THE MEAT FILLING

3 tablespoons olive oil

1 onion, finely diced

1 lb (450 g) ground beef, lamb, or combination of both

1 teaspoon sea salt

1 teaspoon bahārat (Arabic 7-spice mix)

2 teaspoons ground sumac

1 teaspoon dried marjoram

½ teaspoon ground cumin

½ teaspoon ground black pepper

½ teaspoon Aleppo pepper or red pepper flakes

2 tablespoons roasted pine nuts

Let's start by preparing the meat filling. Heat a large frying pan over medium heat, add the oil, and sauté the onion for a couple of minutes to soften. Add the meat, stir to break it up, and cook until lightly browned and crumbly, 8–10 minutes. Add the salt and spices to the mixture and continue to sauté for another 2 minutes to bring out the flavors of the spices. Once everything is cooked, add the pine nuts, turn off the heat, and set aside to cool.

To make the potato and bulgur coating, bring the water to a boil in a large pot over medium-high heat, add the potatoes, and cook until they become tender, about 15 minutes. Remove the potatoes using a slotted spoon and let them cool slightly in a large mixing bowl; then, using a potato masher, mash the potatoes until smooth. Gradually add the bulgur wheat and knead it into the mashed potatoes until well combined, about 5 minutes. Add the salt and spices and knead again until the mixture has a dough-like consistency. Taste and adjust the seasoning.

To assemble the kibbeh, fill a small bowl with cold water and keep it handy. Dampen your palms with water and divide the potato and bulgur mixture into 18 small balls weighing about 1¼ oz (35 g) each.

CONTINUED

SALADS AND STARTERS | 35

FOR THE POTATO AND BULGUR COATING

6 cups (1.4 l) water

2 russet potatoes, peeled and quartered

½ lb (225 g) fine brown bulgur wheat, rinsed in cool water and drained

1 teaspoon sea salt

½ teaspoon bahārat (Arabic 7-spice mix)

½ teaspoon ground cumin

¼ teaspoon ground turmeric

¼ teaspoon ground black pepper

½ teaspoon dried marjoram

½ teaspoon dried mint

4 cups (960 ml) neutral oil

Cradle one ball of the potato and bulgur mixture in the palm of one hand, lightly securing it with your fingers. Dip the index finger of your other hand in water, and then use this wet finger to create a hole in the center of the ball. Gently rotate your finger while pressing toward the sides of the ball to create a cavity big enough to easily fit 1 tablespoon of the meat filling.

Spoon about 1 tablespoon of the meat filling into the cavity. Seal it by moistening your finger in water and using it to smooth the outside of the kibbeh, shaping it into a tiny football while ensuring an even surface. Place the shaped kibbeh on parchment paper and repeat the process with the remaining kibbeh balls.

Heat the oil in a deep skillet or pot to about 350°F (180°C). Fry the kibbeh in batches over medium heat until golden brown, 2–3 minutes per batch, placing them in and removing them from the oil with a slotted spoon. Serve the kibbeh while they are warm, accompanied by a side of salad or yogurt.

NOTES

Give yourself plenty of time to assemble the kibbeh. At the end, you should have small, delicate parcels that are shaped like footballs or elongated eggs with slightly pointed ends. For optimal results, ensure the oil is heated to the correct temperature and fry only a few kibbeh at a time to maintain their integrity. Kibbeh can be prepared in advance and frozen until ready to cook.

Bahārat, the Arabic 7-spice mix, can be purchased at West Asian markets or from online retailers.

CHAPTER 2

SOUPS AND ĀSHES

Chilled Pea and Lettuce Soup • **V GF**
43

Potato and Herb Egg Drop Soup • **V GF**
Āsh Gholvat • 45

Creamy Smoked Fish and Vegetable Soup • **GF**
Cullen Skink • 46

Barley Soup with Beans and Herbs • **V**
Āsh Jo • 48

Bean Soup with Herbs and Noodles • **V**
Āsh Reshteh • 51

Creamy Parsnip and Apple Soup • **VG GF**
53

Fenugreek Soup with Poached Eggs • **V**
Eshkeneh • 55

V • VEGETARIAN   **VG** • VEGAN   **GF** • GLUTEN FREE

THE POINTED GUN

TEHRAN, IRAN | 1979–1983

Everything changed in 1979. With the Iranian Revolution, my carefree childhood gave way to a time of change and uncertainty that reshaped the course of my existence. Each day seemed to introduce new restrictions and regulations as the country grappled to find its new identity. Overnight, every aspect of daily life became unpredictable, bringing tension and apprehension to even simple routines.

Within families, the revolution created rifts and conflicts as differing ideologies clashed. Relatives who once shared close bonds found themselves on opposing sides, leading to strained interactions and fractured relationships. Conversations became tense, laced with caution and guarded opinions. The harmony and sense of connection that once existed within our circle suddenly seemed distant and unattainable. As the years passed, the once tightly knit fabric of my extended family unraveled, leaving an irreparable void. Gone were the carefree gatherings in Daryakenar.

The revolution also brought about drastic changes in food and eating habits. Rations, coupons, and long lines replaced the previous abundance and made it hard to obtain even everyday ingredients. Celebrations became more restricted; shortages limited visits to avoid imposing oneself on the host. Despite the strong tradition of generosity, one had to be mindful of the week's allotment for one's own family before offering to share meals.

Amid this backdrop of profound changes in every aspect of Iran's landscape, I entered my teenage years.

Also at this time, my mother was experiencing some health issues, so I tried to contribute to the daily cooking tasks. I discovered that I could whip up simple dishes. Making an Iranian-style omelet or the stew known as bij bij became routine. However, I did discover that there is such a thing as too much turmeric! Out of necessity, my previously limited experience with cooking took on a different shape. This would lay the foundation for me to associate food with care and love, and became an important part of my identity.

> *I'm still coping with my trauma, but coping by trying to find different ways to heal it rather than hide it.*
>
> —CLEMANTINE WAMARIYA

Cooking was not the only daily routine that underwent drastic change. Strict regulations dictated what we could do in public and even how we lived in our private spaces. Secrecy became the norm, and we had to be cautious about every move we made. Nighttime became particularly daunting, as frequent car stops and checks imposed a sense of fear and intrusion.

When the war with Iraq broke out in 1980, our lives took an even more unsettling turn. The sound of sirens became the new norm, and we found ourselves seeking shelter in our inadequate basement. Power outages became commonplace, replacing the once-familiar atmosphere of dinner parties and the freedom to celebrate life.

The third anniversary of the US embassy hostage-taking—November 4, 1982—has become a truly defining moment in my life. On that day, my classmates and I were abruptly pulled out of school and taken to a nearby mosque. Little did we know that this prayer session was a prelude to something much more significant. We were soon joined by other students and forced into a procession to demonstrate outside the US embassy.

The tension was palpable. After the revolution, my family had resolved that, if possible, I would leave Iran and move to the United States. But here I was, forced to chant sentiments of animosity toward the country I would one day call home. This conflict led me to make a decision: I separated myself from the march, determined to escape.

My hopes were quickly shattered when I was captured by a boy soldier, not much older than my fifteen-year-old self. He pushed me against a wall, his rifle pointed directly at my chest. He could have done anything to me in that moment. But for whatever reason, the boy soldier eventually lowered his rifle and hurled me back into the line of marchers. To this day, I don't know whether I was being brave or stupid, but a little later, I made another attempt to escape the march, this time successfully.

The opportunity to leave Iran eventually presented itself, but it came with a heavy dose of uncertainty and complex feelings. Leaving meant bidding farewell to more than just a physical place. It presented the notion of never knowing when or even whether I would return. I left with an assortment of feelings: relief that I had the privilege to leave and hope for new beginnings, but also deep loss and a profound sense of uncertainty for the future.

SOUPS AND ĀSHES | 41

ĀSH

The Persian term *āsh* refers to a flavorful and normally thick soup rich in some combination of beans, grains, noodles, herbs, spices, and sometimes meat. There are said to be fifty variations, many associated with specific regions of Iran.

To highlight the importance of āsh in Iranian cuisine, we need a quick Persian language lesson. In old spoken Persian, the word *āsh* meant any kind of prepared food. Combined with the words *paz* (from the verb *pokhtan*, "to cook") and *khāneh* ("home"), *āshpazi* means "cooking," *āshpaz* means "cook" or "chef," and *āshpaz khāneh* means "kitchen." Āsh (the dish) is as central to Iranian cooking as āsh (the word) is to the Persian language.

The finishing touch to many āshes is a selection of toppings that add even more complexity to the dish. Most common are crispy or caramelized onions, garlic, mint, and kashk (fermented whey). I normally use all four, but of course, you can mix and match according to your preferences. These toppings can also be used on spreads, such as kashk kadu on page 76.

You can make your toppings in advance, or while your āsh is cooking.

PIĀZ DĀGH (FRIED ONION)

½ cup (120 ml) olive oil

1 small onion, thinly sliced

¼ teaspoon sea salt

In a large frying pan, combine the olive oil and onion. Sprinkle with the salt and sauté over medium-low heat until the onion turns golden and caramelized, about 20 minutes.

SIR DĀGH (FRIED GARLIC)

2 tablespoons olive oil

6 cloves garlic, thinly sliced

In a small saucepan, heat the olive oil and sauté the garlic over low heat until it becomes golden brown, 1–2 minutes. Be careful not to burn it!

NA'NĀ DĀGH (FRIED MINT)

2 tablespoons olive oil

2 tablespoons dried mint

In a small saucepan, heat the olive oil and add the mint. Sauté over low heat for 30–45 seconds to release its aroma.

KASHK (FERMENTED WHEY)

To make it easy to drizzle over the top of your āsh, simply combine 2 tablespoons kashk with 1 tablespoon water.

CHILLED PEA AND LETTUCE SOUP

MAKES 4 SERVINGS • **V GF**

While this may seem like an unconventional combination of ingredients, this soup has consistently been a crowd-pleaser. Tarragon, a cherished herb in Iran, delivers a delightful blend of licorice and anise flavors. This soup carries a comforting taste reminiscent of home, even though these particular ingredients are not commonly combined in Iranian cuisine.

2 tablespoons olive oil

1 leek, both the green and white parts, thinly sliced

2 cloves garlic, minced

1 lb (450 g) frozen peas

½ teaspoon sea salt

½ teaspoon ground black pepper

3 cups (720 ml) low-sodium vegetable broth or water

1 head romaine lettuce, coarsely chopped

1 cup (240 ml) heavy whipping cream, plus more for serving

½ cup (15 g) chopped fresh tarragon

Heat a Dutch oven over medium-high heat. Once the pot is hot, add the olive oil and then the leek. Reduce the heat to medium-low and gently sauté the leek, stirring frequently. We want to cook the leek slowly until it becomes soft and fragrant, without browning, about 10 minutes.

Toss in the garlic and sauté for 2 minutes.

Now it's time to add the peas, salt, and pepper and pour in the broth. Cover and let the soup simmer over low heat for the peas to brighten and soften; this should take about 5 minutes.

Turn off the heat, add the lettuce, cream, and tarragon and give it a stir.

Carefully transfer the soup in batches to a high-speed blender and process until the soup is well blended and creamy. Pour the soup into a bowl and refrigerate until fully chilled, about 3 hours.

Serve the soup in individual bowls, garnishing each bowl with a drizzle of heavy whipping cream. Serve the soup with a side of crusty bread for dipping.

> **NOTES**
>
> *Although I prefer to serve this soup chilled on hot summer days, it can also be served hot with a hearty slice of sourdough bread.*
>
> *For a vegan version, blend ¼ cup (35 g) macadamia or pine nuts and 1 cup (240 ml) water in a high-speed blender in place of the cream. Add the nut cream earlier, alongside the peas and broth. Cook for 5 minutes before puréeing.*

SOUPS AND ĀSHES

Āsh Gholvat

POTATO AND HERB EGG DROP SOUP

MAKES 4 SERVINGS • V GF

In 2021, during the Covid pandemic, I started demonstrating Iranian dishes on Instagram Live with a friend in Tehran. We experimented with various recipes, and one week, I shared an āsh that I had recently discovered in an old Iranian cookbook. Āsh gholvat is notably lighter and quicker to prepare than other āshes, yet it remains satisfying and full of flavor. Here is my interpretation.

3 cups (720 ml) water

6 cups (360 g) finely chopped fresh spinach

½ cup (15 g) finely chopped fresh parsley

½ cup (15 g) finely chopped fresh cilantro

½ cup (15 g) finely chopped fresh dill

4 green onions, thinly sliced

4 Yukon gold potatoes (about 2 lb/1 kg total), diced into ½-inch (12-mm) cubes

1½ teaspoons sea salt

½ teaspoon ground black pepper

1 teaspoon ground turmeric

1 tablespoon rice flour mixed with 2 tablespoons cool water

4 cups (960 ml) milk

2 eggs, lightly beaten

Toppings (see page 42)

In a large pot, bring the water to a boil. Add the spinach, herbs, and green onions and let them simmer for about 5 minutes. Toss in the potatoes, salt, pepper, turmeric, and rice flour mixture.

Reduce the heat to low, cover, and let it simmer until the potatoes have softened to your liking and the broth has thickened slightly, about 15 minutes.

Pour in the milk, bring the mixture back to a gentle boil, and continue to simmer over low heat for another 5 minutes.

Slowly drizzle the beaten eggs into the āsh without stirring, allowing the eggs to form a silken strand. Turn off the heat and let it stand for 5 minutes, covered.

Place the āsh into a serving bowl and garnish it with the toppings.

NOTES

Since this dish has a relatively fast cooking time, you may want to prepare the optional toppings (see page 42) in advance.

For a deeper flavor, consider substituting chicken or vegetable broth for the water in this soup.

Cullen Skink

CREAMY SMOKED FISH AND VEGETABLE SOUP

MAKES 4 SERVINGS · **GF**

Scotland has captured my heart ever since I married a Scot. Its stunning landscapes, from the rugged Highlands to the peaceful lochs, and its friendly people have become a meaningful part of my life.

In Scotland, as in many countries, thrifty cooks have long found ways to make distinctive, flavorful dishes from readily available local ingredients. Cullen skink was originally one of these "peasant foods." The word *skink* probably comes from the soup's original protein, which was beef hock, but over time meat became too expensive for many. White fish was substituted because it was plentiful in fishing villages—like Cullen on the North Sea coast—and was available year-round because it could be preserved by smoking.

This adaptation is most definitely not traditional, but it delivers the essence of cullen skink in a fresh, colorful bowl.

½ lb (225 g) smoked haddock or other white fish, skin on

1 bay leaf

2 cups (480 ml) low-sodium vegetable broth

2 tablespoons olive oil

1 onion, diced

2 stalks celery, diced

2 carrots, diced

3 potatoes, diced

1 teaspoon sea salt

½ teaspoon ground black pepper

¼ cup (30 g) raw cashews

1 cup (240 ml) water

¼ cup (8 g) finely chopped fresh parsley

Put the fish into a saucepan with the bay leaf, cover with the vegetable broth, and simmer over medium-low heat for 10 minutes. Remove the fish from the pan and set aside to cool. Reserve the cooking liquid.

Heat a pot over medium-low heat, add the oil, and stir in the onion. Cover and sweat the onion without letting it develop any color, about 10 minutes.

Toss in the celery, carrots, and potatoes and lightly sauté for 2 minutes. Add the fish cooking liquid with the bay leaf, salt, and pepper and bring to a simmer. Cover and cook until the vegetables are al dente, 15–20 minutes.

While the soup simmers, remove and discard the skin from the fish and break the flesh into flakes, making sure to remove any and all bones. Then combine the cashews and water in a blender and process on high speed until completely smooth and creamy, 60–90 seconds.

Add the fish and cashew cream to the pot, cover, and simmer for about 5 minutes to meld all the flavors together.

To serve, remove the bay leaf and transfer the soup to a large serving bowl. Garnish with fresh parsley and serve hot.

NOTES

Smoked white fish is not always easy to obtain, but smoked trout or smoked salmon makes a suitable substitute.

Instead of the traditional milk or cream, I've used cashew cream to create a lighter version of this soup, emphasizing the flavors of the vegetables and smoked fish.

Āsh Jo

BARLEY SOUP WITH BEANS AND HERBS

MAKES 6 SERVINGS • V

This āsh comes with a love letter attached! In the mid-2000s, I introduced this soup to a group of staff members at my local co-op, where I taught cooking classes. Many years later, Amelia, a colleague who had since moved to New York and was working at a food website, contacted me with exciting news. She had published an article titled "The Life-Changing Persian Soup I've Been Mastering for 15 Years (and Still Going Strong)."

Amelia wrote, "I knew I loved this humble bowl of soup before it was even placed before me—I could smell it in the air. And when I tasted it, I loved it even more than I thought I would. It was a defining moment in my young cook's heart. That class, fifteen years ago, created a culinary curiosity within me that changed my life and kept me seeking more. I've made this soup so many times that now it has become part of my family's life fabric. My daughters will always have the memory of this soup at our dinner table, and it's possible they love it so much that they will serve it at their own tables, too."

2 tablespoons olive oil

1 large onion, diced

4 cloves garlic, minced

1 teaspoon ground turmeric

2 teaspoons ground cumin

6 cups (1.4 l) low-sodium vegetable broth, plus more as needed

½ cup (100 g) dried chickpeas, soaked overnight and rinsed

¼ cup (50 g) dried red kidney beans, soaked overnight and rinsed

1½ teaspoons sea salt

½ teaspoon ground black pepper

Place a large Dutch oven over medium heat until it warms up. Add the olive oil and sauté the onion until it turns soft and translucent, 5–7 minutes.

Toss the garlic, turmeric, and cumin into the pot and sauté for another 2 minutes, allowing their flavors to meld and infuse into the onion.

Pour the vegetable broth into the pot, add the chickpeas and beans, and bring the mixture to a gentle boil. Once boiling, reduce the heat, cover, and simmer for 45 minutes. If you haven't done so in advance, this is a good time to prepare your toppings (see page 42).

After 45 minutes, season the soup with the salt and pepper and add the barley, rice, and lentils to the pot. Cover and cook over low heat for another 15 minutes.

1 cup (200 g) pearled barley

½ cup (100 g) basmati rice

½ cup (100 g) lentils

4 cups (120 g) coarsely chopped fresh parsley

2 cups (60 g) coarsely chopped fresh cilantro

2 cups (60 g) coarsely chopped fresh dill

1½ cups (90 g) coarsely chopped fresh spinach

1 cup (240 ml) kashk (fermented whey)

Toppings (see page 42)

Toss in the fresh herbs, spinach, and kashk, cover, and cook until the herbs are fully integrated into the soup, about 30 minutes. Be sure to give the soup an occasional stir, and add more broth as needed to prevent anything from sticking to the bottom of the pot. Taste and adjust the seasoning.

Turn off the heat and let the āsh stand for 10 minutes. Transfer the āsh to a large soup bowl and garnish it with the āsh toppings.

NOTES

To save time, you can use canned beans; make sure to rinse and drain them and add them when you introduce the barley.

Sour cream or yogurt is a suitable substitute for kashk (fermented whey).

Āsh Reshteh

BEAN SOUP WITH HERBS AND NOODLES

MAKES 4 SERVINGS • V

As far back as I can recall, I've cherished āsh reshteh—a hearty, stick-to-your-ribs vegetarian soup. Linked to special Iranian celebrations (like Nowruz, the Iranian New Year), the noodles symbolize life's intricate journey.

2 tablespoons olive oil

1 large onion, diced

4 cloves garlic, minced

1 teaspoon ground turmeric

9 cups (2.2 l) low-sodium vegetable broth or water, plus more as needed

⅓ cup (70 g) dried pinto beans, soaked overnight and rinsed

⅓ cup (70 g) dried red kidney beans, soaked overnight and rinsed

⅓ cup (70 g) dried chickpeas, soaked overnight and rinsed

½ cup (100 g) lentils

1½ teaspoons sea salt

½ teaspoon ground black pepper

2 cups (60 g) coarsely chopped fresh parsley

2 cups (60 g) coarsely chopped fresh cilantro

½ cup (15 g) coarsely chopped fresh dill

1 cup (60 g) coarsely chopped fresh spinach

1 small leek or 6 green onions, finely chopped

¼ cup (60 ml) āb ghureh (unripe grape juice)

9 oz (250 g) linguine or reshteh (Iranian noodles), broken into thirds

1 cup (240 ml) kashk (fermented whey)

Heat a large Dutch oven over medium heat, add the olive oil, and sauté the onion until it becomes soft, 5–7 minutes.

Add the garlic and turmeric, sautéing them together with the onion for a couple more minutes.

Pour in the vegetable broth, add the pinto beans, red kidney beans, and chickpeas to the pot, and bring to a gentle boil. Once boiling, reduce the heat to low, cover the pot, and let the beans simmer for 45 minutes. They will be well into their cooking process but still have a bit more to go. If you haven't done so in advance, this is a good time to prepare your toppings (see page 42).

Add the lentils, salt, and pepper. Stir and cook over low heat for 15 minutes.

Stir in the herbs, spinach, leek or green onions, and āb ghureh, keep the heat on low, and cook for an additional 30 minutes to enhance the herbal flavor.

Stir the noodles into the āsh and cook them until they soften, about 15 minutes. Be sure to give the āsh a couple of stirs during this time to make sure that nothing is sticking to the bottom of the pot. As the noodles cook, they will absorb some of the broth. If necessary, add more broth to make sure the āsh doesn't become too dry and maintains enough liquid for cooking the noodles.

CONTINUED

Toppings (see page 42)

Stir in the kashk until it blends completely, giving the dish a creamy and tangy flavor. This is a great time to taste the āsh and adjust the levels of salt and acidity to your liking.

Turn off the heat and let the āsh stand for 10 minutes, letting the flavors settle and come together. Transfer the āsh to a large serving bowl and garnish it with the āsh toppings.

> **NOTES**
>
> *If āb ghureh, unripe grape juice, is not available, lemon juice can serve as a good alternative.*
>
> *Kashk (fermented whey) has a unique flavor profile, combining saltiness and tanginess. Yogurt or sour cream can serve as a suitable substitute.*
>
> *Dried beans add rich flavors and depth to this soup. However, to save time, you can use canned beans instead. Rinse the beans and add them when you add the lentils.*

CREAMY PARSNIP AND APPLE SOUP

MAKES 6 SERVINGS • VG GF

The perfect autumn dinner for me is a hot bowl of creamy soup with a slice of rustic sourdough bread. Due to their starchiness, root vegetables offer luscious textures and earthy flavors. This recipe combines parsnips, apples, and coconut cream, creating a velvety, flavorful soup.

2 tablespoons neutral oil

1 onion, sliced

4 parsnips, sliced ½ inch (12 mm) thick

1 Honeycrisp apple, quartered and cored

2 cloves garlic, minced

1-inch (2.5-cm) piece of fresh ginger, peeled and minced

½ cup (120 ml) sake

2½ cups (600 ml) low-sodium vegetable broth

1 teaspoon sea salt

¼ teaspoon chipotle pepper powder, or to taste

1 can (14 oz/400 g) coconut cream

2 tablespoons chopped fresh parsley

Heat a large Dutch oven over medium-high heat, add the oil, and sauté the onion until it becomes aromatic and translucent, 5–7 minutes. Add the parsnips and continue sautéing for about 5 minutes before adding the apple, garlic, and ginger to the mix. Sauté everything for an additional 2 minutes to layer in more flavor.

Stir the sake into the soup, picking up any flavor buildup from the bottom of the pot before adding the vegetable broth, salt, and chipotle pepper. Cover, reduce the heat to low, and let the soup cook until the parsnips have softened, about 45 minutes.

Stir in the coconut cream. Using either an immersion blender or carefully transferring the soup in batches to a high-speed blender, process until it turns smooth and velvety. Once the entire soup is blended, check its consistency. If it appears too thick, you can add a bit of water. Taste and make any necessary adjustments to the seasonings.

Pour the soup into bowls, garnish with chopped parsley, and serve with crusty sourdough bread.

> **NOTES**
>
> *I generally leave vegetables unpeeled, as the peel enhances their earthy flavors, but I do scrub them thoroughly with a vegetable brush.*
>
> *Try swapping parsnips for carrots, sweet potatoes, or butternut squash. Sake can be replaced with dry white wine or omitted.*

Eshkeneh

FENUGREEK SOUP WITH POACHED EGGS

MAKES 4 SERVINGS • V

Eshkeneh is a classic but unpretentious soup with a short and easy-to-assemble list of ingredients that can be prepared in about thirty minutes. While eshkeneh is often referred to as Iranian onion soup, for me, the true star is fenugreek leaves, with their strong scent and flavor profile.

¼ cup (60 ml) olive oil

2 onions, diced

1 teaspoon ground turmeric

2 large russet potatoes, peeled and cut into ½-inch (12-mm) cubes

1 tablespoon all-purpose flour

2 tablespoons dried fenugreek leaves

4 cups (960 ml) low-sodium chicken or vegetable broth

1 tablespoon tomato paste

2 tomatoes, diced

2 tablespoons fresh lemon juice

1 teaspoon sea salt

½ teaspoon ground black pepper

4 eggs

Place a pot on the stove and turn the heat to medium. Once the pot is heated, drizzle in the olive oil. Add the onions and sauté them until they become translucent, 5–7 minutes.

Sprinkle the turmeric over the onions and sauté for a couple of minutes.

Toss in the diced potatoes and stir to ensure they are coated with the onions and turmeric mixture.

Sprinkle the flour and fenugreek leaves over the potato mixture and stir everything together for another minute.

Pour the chicken broth into the pot, followed by the tomato paste, tomatoes, lemon juice, salt, and pepper. Stir and bring the soup to a gentle simmer, then reduce the heat to low, cover, and cook until the potatoes are softened to your liking, 20–25 minutes. Taste and make any necessary adjustments.

Crack an egg and drop it directly into the soup, allowing it to poach in the broth undisturbed. Repeat this step for each egg, and allow them to poach for about 5 minutes for a soft-boiled consistency.

Ladle the hot soup into bowls, including a poached egg in each, and serve it with a piece of flatbread and pickled vegetables on the side.

> **NOTES**
>
> *To make the soup more filling, toss in some extra veggies like carrots, celery, cabbage, or mushrooms. If you can't find fenugreek, you can replace it with fresh cilantro or parsley leaves and add them at the end.*

CHAPTER 3

KUKUS

Fresh Herb Kuku • **V GF**
Kuku Sabzi • 60

Potato Kuku • **V**
Kuku Sibzamini • 63

Falafel Kuku • **V GF**
64

Walnut Kuku • **V GF**
Kuku Gerdu • 65

Eggplant Kuku • **V GF**
Kuku Bādemjān • 66

V • VEGETARIAN   **GF** • GLUTEN FREE

THE IMMIGRANT LIFE

SEDONA, AZ | 1984

No two immigration stories are the same, and no one can prepare an immigrant for what's to come. Each story will inevitably be filled with its own twists and turns. But underneath the unique details, there's a common thread: a process of integration into a new environment while slowly and subconsciously putting distance between you and your original culture.

After years of anticipation in Tehran and months of waiting in Europe to acquire my visa, I arrived in the United States in 1984, at the age of seventeen. I'd been enrolled in high school in Sedona, Arizona.

Like Isabel Allende, I soon realized that no one cared about the events of my prior life. My childhood in Tehran and by the Caspian Sea—witnessing a revolution at the age of twelve, starting high school on the first day of the Iran-Iraq war, finally leaving Iran—all of these were irrelevant now. I would likely never return to Iran, and America would be my new home.

One of my earliest experiences with food in America demonstrated that I had a lot to learn. In a Chinese restaurant, I was served a bowl of sticky rice. I have since come to appreciate the many ways rice is prepared around the world, but at the time, I didn't know what to think! The only rice I knew was the Iranian version: light and fluffy.

Of course, in high school and university cafeterias, one has to eat what is served or go hungry. I even started to eat tomatoes, celery, spinach, zucchini, and eggplant! There were no more fragrant rice dishes or stews packed with aromatic herbs. Cafeteria food was supplemented with my newfound favorite American sandwich: white bread, mayonnaise, and bologna. I did once dare to cook an Iranian stew of cow's tongue in my dormitory using a slow cooker. The aroma managed to waft through all three floors of the building, and I only escaped detection through the forbearance of a friendly roommate. That experiment was never repeated!

> **I learned very quickly that when you emigrate, you lose the crutches that have been your support; you must begin from zero because the past is erased with a single stroke, and no one cares where you're from or what you did before.**
>
> —ISABEL ALLENDE

My learning curve extended to language, of course. I had studied English diligently in Iran, and had good grammar and knowledge of sentence construction. It rapidly became clear, however, that I lacked two things that were just as important: a complete vocabulary and an American accent. Two particular experiences have remained with me.

58 | BITTER & SWEET

Often, as I attempted to speak English with my high school classmates, I was met with a "Huh?" or a "What?" I can still feel the sensation deep in my belly, a tightening that stemmed from embarrassment and shame: I spoke like a foreigner, and was constantly reminded how different I was from others around me. I needed to learn to speak so well that no one would ever say "Huh?" or "What?" to me again. To this day, these two words are triggering.

A year after this realization, my English teacher smugly announced that his ESL students would likely not achieve anything better than a C grade. This assertion cut through me like a knife. And true enough, he gave us all Cs. His thoughtless words have continued to haunt me all these years as they directly challenged the prospect of making America my home.

In my family, education was highly valued and cherished, but the sciences and practical subjects were definitely emphasized over art and artistic expression. When I attended my very first theater performance at university, I was mesmerized: I had never before seen a live performance. Decades later, watching my friends' daughter perform in a high school production of Macbeth, I realized that I had simply never made time for art or creativity in my life. I had been too busy learning a new language and assimilating into my adopted culture.

Human resilience is quite extraordinary. We can make brilliantly difficult decisions when our future is at stake. But survival comes at a cost. I can now see how that affected my life: I became so focused on fitting in that I stopped speaking Persian, celebrating Iranian holidays, and eating Iranian food.

Though I didn't realize it at the time, I was steadily letting go of my ties to my roots and culture.

KUKU

Kuku is a versatile egg-based dish that shares some similarities with the Italian frittata or the Spanish tortilla. Frittata and tortilla tend to lead with the eggs but incorporate other ingredients. In contrast, kuku first emphasizes other ingredients— generally mixtures of herbs and vegetables, but sometimes meat—which are bound together by the eggs.

The ingredients incorporated into kuku may be raw or partially cooked in advance, depending on their texture. The most common spices are salt, pepper, and turmeric, but regional and family traditions introduce others. Since eggs readily absorb flavor, feel free to experiment with spices when preparing kuku.

Kuku can take two forms: It can be cooked as a whole, circular dish, or shaped and cooked individually, similar to patties or croquettes.

Typically, kuku is cooked in a frying pan with a lid. While a nonstick pan works particularly well, a regular cast-iron or stainless steel pan can also do the job, provided you use extra care when cooking and removing the kuku from the pan. Alternatively, you can prepare kuku in a lightly greased oven-safe baking dish.

Kuku can be served for breakfast, lunch, dinner, or as a light snack. It pairs well with steamed rice and traditional sides like pickled vegetables, yogurt, or a platter of fresh herbs. Alternatively, kuku makes an excellent base for a sandwich or wrap, combined with leafy greens, tomatoes, cucumbers, and pickles.

Kuku Sabzi

FRESH HERB KUKU

MAKES 4 SERVINGS • **V GF**

Kuku sabzi is a delightful masterpiece, bursting with contrasting, vibrant flavors. The freshness and fragrance of the herb medley are accentuated by the crunch of walnuts and the tangy brightness of barberries. When fried perfectly, kuku sabzi offers a lightly crispy outer layer while retaining a moist and savory essence. It can be enjoyed as an appetizer or a main course.

- 2 cups (60 g) fresh cilantro
- 2 cups (60 g) fresh parsley
- 2 cups (60 g) fresh dill
- 1 cup (30 g) nira (garlic chives)
- ¼ cup (25 g) walnuts, coarsely chopped
- 3 tablespoons barberries, rinsed
- 1 tablespoon dried fenugreek leaves
- 1½ teaspoons sea salt
- ½ teaspoon ground black pepper
- ½ teaspoon ground turmeric
- 5 eggs
- 6 tablespoons (90 ml) neutral oil, divided

Begin by processing the fresh herbs and nira in a food processor until they're coarsely chopped. Transfer to a large mixing bowl. Add the walnuts, barberries, fenugreek leaves, salt, pepper, and turmeric to the bowl and blend with a whisk or a fork. Add the eggs one by one and whisk until you have a batter that's just wet enough to pour but is still dense with herbs. You should not be able to see any eggs separating from the batter.

Heat a nonstick frying pan over medium heat. Pour 4 tablespoons (60 ml) of the oil into the pan. After the oil has spread and is lightly shimmering, pour the entire kuku mixture into the pan. Gently shake the pan until the mixture is evenly spread out.

Cover and cook the kuku until the mixture is firm enough to flip over, about 15 minutes. Place a large plate, inverted, over the pan and carefully flip the kuku onto the plate. Then add the remaining 2 tablespoons of oil and slide the kuku back into the pan. Alternatively, you can cut the kuku into quarters and flip each piece individually. Cook the kuku uncovered for another 10 minutes. Serve kuku sabzi with flatbread and yogurt.

> **NOTES**
>
> *Nira (garlic chives) are typically found in Asian markets. Chives, leeks, or green onions are excellent substitutes.*
>
> *You can bake kuku sabzi in your oven instead of cooking it on the stovetop. Use a 9-inch (23-cm) pie dish or similar oven-proof baking dish and butter the inside before pouring in the batter. Bake at 375°F (190°C) until the eggs are fully cooked, about 30 minutes.*

Kuku Sibzamini

POTATO KUKU

MAKES 4 SERVINGS • V

Potato patties, such as pancakes and latkes, feature in many cuisines worldwide. Kuku sibzamini is an Iranian version, combining potatoes and eggs with a touch of herbs and spices. They are fried until soft on the inside and crispy on the outside, resulting in a delectable medley of textures and flavors.

4 russet potatoes (about 2 lb/1 kg)

1 small onion, grated, with the juices squeezed out

2 eggs, beaten

2 tablespoons bread crumbs, or more as needed

2 teaspoons dried mint

1 teaspoon ground turmeric

1 teaspoon sea salt

½ teaspoon ground black pepper

½ cup (120 ml) neutral oil, divided

In a large pot, cover the potatoes with water and bring to a boil over medium heat. Cover the pot and continue boiling until they're almost fully cooked but you can still feel some resistance when you insert a paring knife, about 20 minutes. Remove the potatoes with a slotted spoon and let them cool before peeling. Grate them into a large mixing bowl, add the onion, eggs, bread crumbs, and spices and mix well. Watch out for the consistency of the batter; the potato mixture should not be too wet or sticky. If needed, adjust by adding more bread crumbs.

Dampen your hands and shape the mixture into small round patties, each 3-4 inches (7.5-10 cm) wide and no more than ½ inch (12 mm) thick. To avoid overcrowding the pan, cook the patties in two batches. Heat a large frying pan over medium heat, add ¼ cup (60 ml) of the oil, and once it's hot, fry half of the patties until they're golden brown and lightly crispy, 4-5 minutes per side. Remove the patties from the pan and let them drain on paper towels to remove excess oil. Repeat the process with the remaining patties and oil.

Kuku is best served with flatbread and a side of fresh herbs, tomatoes, and yogurt.

NOTES

For additional flavor and color, grind ½ teaspoon of saffron threads, mix them with 1 tablespoon of hot water, and add them to the batter.

You can make this kuku in one large batch instead of individual patties. Pour all of the potato batter into an oiled nonstick frying pan, cover, and cook over medium heat for 15 minutes. Then, carefully flip it, add more oil, and cook uncovered until a light crust forms on the bottom, about 10 minutes.

FALAFEL KUKU

MAKES 4 SERVINGS • **V GF**

I've always loved chickpeas in any form, my two favorites being crispy falafel and creamy hummus. This dish combines both of them into an Iranian favorite, kuku, resulting in what I call falafel kuku. The soft, creamy interior and delicate, crispy shell feature all the familiar flavors.

1 can (15 oz/425 g) chickpeas, rinsed and drained

1 small onion, quartered

4 cloves garlic, chopped

⅓ cup (80 g) tahini

1 teaspoon sea salt

1 teaspoon red pepper flakes

1 tablespoon cumin seeds

1 teaspoon ground coriander

¼ cup (8 g) fresh parsley

¼ cup (8 g) fresh cilantro

2 tablespoons fresh lemon juice

1 tablespoon lemon zest

6 eggs

6 tablespoons (90 ml) olive oil, divided

Place all of the ingredients except the eggs and oil into a food processor and pulse until coarsely chopped.

Grab a large mixing bowl and whisk the eggs. Add the chickpea mixture to the eggs, whisk well to combine, and set aside.

Heat a nonstick frying pan over medium heat before adding 4 tablespoons (60 ml) of the olive oil. Carefully but quickly pour the chickpea mixture into the pan.

Give the pan a good shake to spread the mixture out. Cover and cook the kuku until it's firm and forms a golden crust on the bottom, about 15 minutes.

Place a large plate, inverted, over the pan, then carefully flip the pan over to transfer the kuku onto the plate. Add the remaining 2 tablespoons of oil to the pan and then gently slide the kuku back into the pan. Alternatively, you can cut the kuku into quarters and flip each piece individually.

Continue to cook the kuku uncovered over medium heat to develop a light crust on the bottom, about 10 minutes.

Slide onto a serving platter and serve with flatbread, a side of plain yogurt, and sālād shirāzi (see page 30).

Kuku Gerdu

WALNUT KUKU

MAKES 4 SERVINGS • V GF

Kuku gerdu illustrates the remarkable power of food to forge connections. While we've never met in person, my friend Leila Nabizadeh and I bonded on social media over our shared passion for Caspian Sea regional cuisine. Leila introduced me to this beloved dish from her ancestral home in the stunning Gilan province, and it quickly became a favorite in my own home.

1 Yukon gold potato

1 cup (100 g) walnuts

½ cup (15 g) fresh parsley

¼ cup (8 g) fresh dill

¼ cup (8 g) fresh mint

¼ cup (8 g) fresh chives

2 cloves garlic, minced

1 small onion, grated

1 teaspoon sea salt

½ teaspoon ground black pepper

1 teaspoon ground turmeric

5 large eggs

6 tablespoons (90 ml) neutral oil, divided

Place the potato in a small pan with enough water to cover it. Bring it to a boil, reduce the heat to low, cover, and cook until it's nice and soft, about 15 minutes. Remove the potato from the water, let it cool down, and then grate it into a mixing bowl. Process the walnuts in a food processor until they're finely ground, being careful to stop before they turn into walnut butter. Add the walnuts to the mixing bowl. Next, process the herbs and garlic in the same food processor until they're finely chopped. Combine these, along with the onion, salt, pepper, and turmeric, in the mixing bowl and give everything a good stir.

In another mixing bowl, whisk the eggs and then combine them with all of the other ingredients in the main bowl.

Heat a nonstick frying pan over medium heat. Add 4 tablespoons (60 ml) of the oil and wait until it begins to spread and lightly shimmer before pouring the entire kuku mixture into the pan. Shake the pan until the mixture is evenly spread out. Cover and cook the kuku until it sets. You should be able to gently press the top surface and feel confident that it's firm enough to flip, which typically takes about 15 minutes.

To flip the kuku, place a large plate, inverted, over the pan, carefully flip the whole kuku onto the plate, then add the remaining 2 tablespoons of oil to the pan and slide the kuku back in. Alternatively, you can make it easier by cutting it into quarters in the pan and flip each piece individually with a spatula. Cook this side of the kuku uncovered for 10 minutes to create a light crust on the bottom. Serve with flatbread, a bundle of fresh herbs, and yogurt.

Kuku Bādemjān

EGGPLANT KUKU

MAKES 4 SERVINGS • **V GF**

I can't help smiling when I think about this dish, recalling my childhood in Iran. I used to expertly maneuver around the eggplant, skillfully avoiding it, and savoring only the eggs. I've outgrown this practice in adulthood, and now embrace the full experience of both elements!

2 Chinese eggplants, peeled and sliced into ¼-inch (6-mm) rounds

½ cup plus 2 tablespoons (150 ml) olive oil, divided, plus more as needed

1½ teaspoons sea salt, divided

1 small onion, thinly sliced

1 small Anaheim pepper, finely diced

1 small red chile pepper, minced, or to taste

2 cloves garlic, minced

1 teaspoon unsalted butter

6 eggs

½ teaspoon ground black pepper

1 teaspoon ground turmeric

Preheat the oven to 400°F (200°C).

Place the eggplants in a large mixing bowl and add ½ cup (120 ml) of the oil and ½ teaspoon of the salt. Toss everything thoroughly to ensure the eggplants are evenly coated.

Arrange the eggplants in a single layer on a baking sheet and roast until they turn golden brown and soften, about 30 minutes. Remember to flip them halfway through, and if necessary, add a bit more oil. Once done, remove the eggplants from the oven and set them aside. Reduce the oven temperature to 375°F (190°C).

As the eggplants are roasting, you can prepare the onion and peppers. Heat a small frying pan over medium heat and add the remaining 2 tablespoons of olive oil. Sauté the onion until it is lightly golden, about 10 minutes. Add the peppers and garlic and continue to sauté for 2 minutes. Remove from the heat and set aside.

Butter a 9-inch (23 cm) pie dish or a similar oven-proof baking dish.

In a large mixing bowl, whisk together the eggs and the remaining 1 teaspoon of salt, the pepper, and the turmeric. Stir in the eggplants, onion, peppers, and garlic and gently toss everything together. Pour the mixture into your prepared baking dish. Place in the oven and bake until the egg mixture is fully cooked and has turned a beautiful golden color, 20–30 minutes.

Remove from the oven and allow it to rest in the dish for about 5 minutes. Gently run a knife around the edges to loosen, then carefully transfer the kuku to a platter using a large spatula.

Serve your kuku with flatbread, fresh herbs, and a dollop of yogurt.

CHAPTER 4

VEGETABLE DISHES

Grilled Corn with Tahini Chimichurri Sauce • **VG GF**
Balāl • 72

Braised Japanese Eggplant • **V**
74

Butternut Squash Spread with Whey and Mint • **V GF**
Kashk Kadu • 76

Braised Burdock with Carrots • **VG**
Kinpira Gobo • 79

Afghan Mushroom Curry • **VG GF**
Samārogh • 80

Roasted Carrots with Feta Sumac Spread • **V GF**
83

Roasted Sunchokes with Cucumber Yogurt Spread • **V GF**
84

Cauliflower Steaks with Creamy Tomato Sauce • **V**
86

V • VEGETARIAN **VG** • VEGAN **GF** • GLUTEN FREE

AN AMERICAN IDENTITY

SEATTLE, WA | 1993

I earned my degree in microbiology in Arizona, but it made sense to pursue a career somewhere with a more vibrant biotech industry. Stepping off the plane in Seattle for a job interview, I could tell that my life was about to change. This city was unlike anything I had ever experienced before. The overcast sky, light rainfall, and refreshing temperature gave me a sense of comfort, while the sound of '90s grunge music stirred something within me.

Seattle became my sanctuary, a place where I would continue to grow and eventually embrace a new identity. Immersed in the Pacific Northwest, I grew my hair, adorned myself in flannel shirts, and pursued my career. Seattle was the first place I had actually chosen to live in, and it provided the first taste of true agency in my life. It will forever occupy a special corner of my heart as the city that empowered me to evolve into the person I became, far removed from the land of my birth.

During this period, I underwent a further transformation in my relationship with food. Having become increasingly uneasy about the conditions in which animals were treated in most food production, I adopted a vegetarian lifestyle. (I have now incorporated some animal products back into my diet, but on a limited and quite selective basis.)

As I delved deeper into my new life, I departed further from my Iranian roots. I had previously maintained some connections with Iranian friends, but as I forged friendships within my new community I began to suppress my Iranian identity. Despite my physical appearance and accent, I was living my life as if I had been born in the United States, adhering to an American life script.

My only Iranian contact in Seattle was a cousin whom I hadn't seen in decades. I did visit with her a few times, the last of which was on a Sizdah Bedar, a holiday marking the thirteenth day of the Iranian New Year. On this special day in spring, Iranians gather outdoors, near a lake or river if possible. They come prepared with all the essentials for brewing tea, along with sweets, fruits, nuts, and special dishes rich in aromatic herbs.

As I did my best to engage in all the activities and conversations—it had been a decade since I last took part in this tradition—I couldn't help but feel a profound detachment from the occasion. The customs that used to be familiar and comforting now seemed remote and irrelevant. That moment was a turning point: leaving the celebration felt like an emotional detachment from Iran, a conscious decision to disconnect.

During the months and years that followed, I shut Iran out of my life as completely as I could. The only communication I maintained was with my parents, and that revolved around updates on our health and daily routines. This self-imposed disconnection felt liberating: I no longer had to confront complex emotions, relive traumatic memories, or grapple with the weight of my history.

> *I long, as does every human being, to be at home wherever I find myself.*
>
> —DR. MAYA ANGELOU

My focus became powerfully clear and singular: to live my American life to the fullest. I embraced weekly gatherings with friends for must-see TV on Thursday nights, joyfully decorated Christmas trees, cooked veggie burgers and veggie dogs on the Fourth of July, and cheered passionately for my local basketball team. Traveling up and down the West Coast to see my musical idol, the quintessentially American Pat Benatar, became a constant in my life, an annual tradition that continues to this day!

Iran did resurface in my life for a while, after I learned in a 2 a.m. phone call that my father had passed away. A wave of grief and loss engulfed me that felt insurmountable at the time. There was no possibility of returning to Iran for the funeral, and conversations turned toward planning my mother's move from Iran to the United States. Once she had immigrated and established herself, my ties to Iran diminished even further. I picked up where I had left off, embracing the new life that I had built.

It wasn't until years later that I read Marjan Kamali's description of an Iranian-American living "on the hyphen." It resonated deeply. To this day I find myself on the hyphen, sometimes struggling, sometimes getting knocked off, and sometimes finding a balance.

Balāl

GRILLED CORN WITH TAHINI CHIMICHURRI SAUCE

MAKES 4 SERVINGS • **VG GF**

Sweet corn, *balāl* in Persian, will always evoke memories of the corn vendors along the roadsides near the Caspian Sea. They would skillfully shuck ears of locally grown corn right before your eyes, grill them to perfection over charcoal, and dip them in intensely salted water.

In this recipe, I've chosen to forgo the brine dunk in favor of a sauce that's bursting with flavor.

- ½ cup (15 g) fresh parsley
- ½ cup (15 g) fresh cilantro
- ⅓ cup (80 ml) red wine vinegar
- ¼ cup (60 g) tahini
- 1 tablespoon fresh oregano
- 2 cloves garlic
- 2 small shallots
- 1 teaspoon sea salt
- 1 small red chile pepper
- ¼ cup (60 ml) olive oil
- 4 ears of corn, husked

First, preheat your grill to high heat.

While the grill is heating up, prepare the sauce. Combine all of the ingredients except the oil and corn in a food processor bowl. Pulse the mixture until coarsely chopped, about 10 pulses. Pour in the oil and pulse a couple more times to combine. Remove the mixture from the bowl and set it aside.

Place the corn on the grill over direct heat and turn it periodically until the kernels are tender and the outside has a nice, blistered, lightly charred appearance, 8–12 minutes.

To serve, place the grilled corn on a platter and generously pour the sauce over it.

> **NOTES**
>
> *This recipe makes a tasty side dish to complement your barbecue, whether you're grilling steak, chicken, or tofu!*

BRAISED JAPANESE EGGPLANT

MAKES 4 SERVINGS • V

Maybe I had a debt to settle for the countless times I dismissed eggplant during my childhood. If so, I think I redeemed myself during my years of instructing plant-based classes, when I consistently featured dishes with eggplant to demonstrate braising techniques. While the eggplant remained a constant, I experimented extensively with options for seasonings, salt, and choices of braising liquid.

Much to my joy, this culinary exploration often received appreciation, even winning over the hearts of many individuals who, like me, had previously struggled to embrace eggplant!

FOR THE VEGAN DASHI

1 cup (240 ml) water

2 dried shiitake mushrooms, broken into small pieces

2-inch (5-cm) piece of kombu (kelp)

To make the dashi, combine the water, mushrooms, and kombu in a small bowl. Cover and let it stand for at least 1 hour or up to 4 hours. Strain the liquid, discard the mushrooms and kombu, and set it aside.

To prepare the eggplants, heat a large frying pan over high heat and add ¼ cup (60 ml) of the neutral oil. Once the oil is hot and shimmering, carefully place half of the eggplants in a single layer in the pan and reduce the heat to medium-low. Allow the eggplants to cook undisturbed on one side until nicely browned, 8–10 minutes. Flip the eggplants, add 2 tablespoons of the oil, and brown the other side, another 5 minutes. Transfer the eggplants to a paper towel–lined plate and repeat the process with the remaining eggplants and neutral oil.

In the same pan, heat the sesame oil over medium heat. When hot, add the shallot, ginger, and garlic and cook, stirring frequently until they become aromatic and slightly browned, about 5 minutes.

FOR THE EGGPLANTS

¾ cup (180 ml) neutral oil, divided

3 Japanese eggplants (about 21 oz/600 g), cut diagonally into ½-inch (12-mm)-thick slices

2 tablespoons toasted sesame oil

1 large shallot, thinly sliced

1-inch (2.5-cm) piece of fresh ginger, peeled and minced

2 cloves garlic, minced

3 tablespoons tamari

2 tablespoons light molasses

1½ tablespoons rice vinegar

¼ cup (60 ml) sake

¼ cup (8 g) coarsely chopped fresh cilantro

1 green onion, thinly sliced diagonally

Return the eggplants to the pan and pour in the tamari, molasses, rice vinegar, sake, and dashi. Raise the heat to high until the braising liquid reaches a gentle simmer. Then, cover the pan, reduce the heat to low, and allow the eggplants to simmer until they become tender and the braising liquid reduces by half, 10–15 minutes. Be sure to taste and make any necessary seasoning adjustments.

To serve, arrange the eggplants on a platter, drizzle with the braising liquid, and garnish with the cilantro and green onions. Serve with a bowl of rice or over your favorite noodles.

NOTES

Traditional dashi or mushroom broth can replace vegan dashi, and you can use white wine instead of sake.

Kashk Kadu

BUTTERNUT SQUASH SPREAD WITH WHEY AND MINT

MAKES 4 SERVINGS • **V GF**

Autumn is my favorite season. As the leaves undergo their stunning transformation, I find myself reminiscing about the vibrant fall foliage in my three cherished cities—Tehran, Boulder, and Seattle—each a unique home to me. However, what I love the most about fall is its bountiful harvest and its array of delicious produce. Squashes, persimmons, quinces, and pomegranates take center stage as the autumnal favorites that remind me of the flavors of Iran.

This dish bears a resemblance to a beloved Iranian eggplant spread known as kashk bādemjān, but swaps out eggplant for butternut squash.

1 large butternut squash (2½–3 lb/1.1–1.4 kg)

¼ cup (60 ml) plus 1 tablespoon olive oil, divided

1½ teaspoons sea salt, divided

1 large onion, thinly sliced

4 cloves garlic, minced

1 teaspoon ground turmeric

1 cup (100 g) walnuts, finely ground

¼ teaspoon cayenne pepper

½ cup (120 ml) kashk (fermented whey)

Toppings (see page 42)

Preheat the oven to 400°F (200°C).

Carefully slice your butternut squash in half with a sharp, sturdy knife. Use a spoon to remove the seeds from the center. Rub the flesh with 1 tablespoon of the oil and sprinkle it with 1 teaspoon of the salt, then place both halves face down on a baking sheet. Roast the squash until the flesh is completely soft when you test it with a fork, up to 1 hour.

Prepare the toppings (see page 42) and the additional ingredients for the spread while the squash is roasting.

Heat a large frying pan over medium heat, add the remaining ¼ cup (60 ml) of oil, and sauté the onion until golden and lightly caramelized, 12–15 minutes.

Stir in the garlic and turmeric, sautéing for 2 minutes, then add the ground walnuts and stir for another 2 minutes to enhance their flavor.

Once the butternut squash is fully baked and soft, remove it from the oven. Use a spoon to scoop out the squash and add it to the pan with the onion and walnut mixture. Sprinkle the remaining ½ teaspoon of salt and the cayenne pepper over the mixture and add the kashk. Toss everything together, ensuring all of the ingredients are well mixed. You can use a potato masher if you wish to create a smoother texture.

Cover the pan, reduce the heat to low, and cook to allow the flavors to meld together, about 10 minutes.

Transfer the spread to a serving platter and garnish with the toppings. Serve with flatbread and a medley of fresh herbs.

> **NOTES**
>
> *Whole milk Greek yogurt or sour cream can be used in place of the kashk (fermented whey).*

Kinpira Gobo

BRAISED BURDOCK WITH CARROTS

MAKES 4 SERVINGS · VG

Attending culinary school proved to be an eye-opening experience, introducing me to a diverse range of vegetables and ingredients while deepening my understanding of culinary techniques and the profound influence of food on our well-being.

One new food item that left an indelible mark on me was burdock, known as *gobo* in Japanese. Burdock is a remarkable specimen: a long, slender root that can reach up to a yard (1 m) in length, with a rugged brown exterior and a crisp white interior.

While it shares superficial similarities with the carrot, burdock delves much deeper into the earth, reaching parts of the soil that carrots can only dream of. With its capacity to root itself deeply into the soil, it's my go-to choice when I need to calm my agitated nervous system and anchor myself.

2 tablespoons toasted sesame oil

12-inch (30-cm) piece of burdock root, cut into thin matchsticks

2 carrots, cut into thin matchsticks

¼ cup (60 ml) vegan dashi (see page 74) or water

2 tablespoons soy sauce

2 tablespoons sake

2 tablespoons mirin (sweet rice vinegar)

1 tablespoon sugar

1 green onion, thinly sliced diagonally

1 teaspoon white sesame seeds

1 small red chile pepper, thinly sliced, or to taste

Heat a frying pan over medium heat, add the oil, and sauté the burdock until it starts to take on some color, about 5 minutes. Toss in the carrots and sauté for another 2 minutes.

Add the dashi, soy sauce, sake, mirin, and sugar. Cook, stirring, until about half of the liquid has evaporated, another couple of minutes.

Transfer to a serving bowl and top with the green onions, sesame seeds, and red chile pepper.

NOTES

I have to acknowledge that burdock is in no way a part of Iranian cuisine. So much so that when my mother visited and encountered this unfamiliar root, she asked me why I was stashing tree branches in my fridge.

While not everything easily transcends cultures, I firmly believe that there's much to gain from acquainting ourselves with other traditions and broadening our culinary horizons.

VEGETABLE DISHES | 79

Samārogh

AFGHAN MUSHROOM CURRY

MAKES 4 SERVINGS • VG GF

I have always been fond of mushrooms and enjoy experimenting with various techniques to highlight their unique and beautiful texture and flavor profile. This particular dish is one I have showcased at fundraising events to support Afghan refugees. Its exquisite layers of flavor have officially elevated it to become my ultimate favorite among mushroom dishes.

⅓ cup (80 ml) neutral oil

4 cloves garlic, coarsely chopped

1 small red chile pepper, seeded, thinly sliced

1 onion, diced

1 teaspoon ground turmeric

1 tablespoon tomato paste

4 tomatoes (about 2 lb/ 1 kg total), quartered

¼ cup (60 ml) water

1½ teaspoons sea salt

4 cups (360 g) oyster mushrooms, shredded

1 teaspoon char masala (see Afghan rice pilaf with lamb, page 115)

¼ cup (8 g) coarsely chopped fresh cilantro

Heat a large frying pan over medium heat, add the oil, and sauté the garlic and red chile pepper for 30 seconds. Add the onion and sauté until translucent, 5–7 minutes. Now add the turmeric and tomato paste, continuing to sauté to layer in more flavors, about 2 minutes. Finally, add the tomatoes, water, and salt. Cover, reduce the heat to low, and cook until the tomatoes have completely softened, about 15 minutes.

Pour the tomato mixture into a blender and blend until smooth. Return the sauce to the pan, adding the mushrooms and char masala. Stir and bring the mixture to a gentle simmer over low heat. Cover and cook until the mushrooms have released their moisture into the sauce and become tender, about 20 minutes. Taste and make any necessary seasoning adjustments.

Transfer the mushroom curry to a serving bowl. Garnish with the cilantro and serve alongside steamed basmati rice.

> **NOTES**
>
> *To add variety in textures and flavors, consider experimenting with various types of mushrooms.*

ROASTED CARROTS WITH FETA SUMAC SPREAD

MAKES 4 SERVINGS • V GF

Roasting carrots seals in their flavor, intensifies their natural sugars, and leaves them tender on the inside and crispy on the outside. The savory, tangy feta sumac spread pairs perfectly with the sweetness of the roasted carrots, making this a great side dish for any meal.

FOR THE CARROTS

8 carrots (about 1½ lb/ 680 g total)

2 tablespoons olive oil

1 teaspoon apple cider vinegar

½ teaspoon sea salt

¼ teaspoon chipotle pepper powder

½ teaspoon ground cumin

1 teaspoon ground sumac

FOR THE FETA DRESSING

¼ lb (115 g) feta cheese

⅓ cup (80 ml) European-style yogurt

2 tablespoons fresh lemon juice

1 tablespoon olive oil

1 clove garlic

¼ teaspoon ground black pepper

FOR THE TOPPING

2 tablespoons toasted pine nuts

2 dates, chopped

2 teaspoons ground sumac

2 tablespoons chopped fresh parsley

Preheat the oven to 400°F (200°C).

To prepare the carrots, cut them in half lengthwise to give them a bit more surface area for caramelization and to get them to cook faster. In a large mixing bowl, whisk together the remaining ingredients. Then add the carrots and—using your hands—toss them until they're fully coated.

Lay the carrots out on a baking sheet in a single layer with the cut side down. Roast them until they are golden and have become crisp and tender, 20-25 minutes. Be sure to flip them once.

To make the feta dressing, while the carrots are roasting, pull out your food processor, add the ingredients, and process until you have a smooth and creamy mixture.

Spread the feta mixture onto a serving platter. Arrange the carrots on top, and then sprinkle with the pine nuts, dates, sumac, and parsley.

ROASTED SUNCHOKES WITH CUCUMBER YOGURT SPREAD

MAKES 4 SERVINGS • V GF

I fell in love with sunchokes at first sight. These peculiar-looking tubers can be roasted to perfection, achieving a golden crispiness on the outside while maintaining a creamy and tender center.

Here's a playful fusion of one of my favorite root vegetables with a classic Iranian side dish, māst-o khiār. This minty cucumber yogurt spread takes the humble sunchoke to new heights.

FOR THE SUNCHOKES

2 lb (1 kg) sunchokes, cut into ¼-inch (6-mm)-thick slices

3 tablespoons neutral oil

½ teaspoon sea salt

¼ teaspoon chipotle pepper powder

1 teaspoon cumin seeds

½ teaspoon aniseed

FOR THE MĀST-O KHIĀR

½ cup (120 ml) whole milk yogurt

1 Persian cucumber, grated

¼ teaspoon dried mint

¼ teaspoon sea salt

⅛ teaspoon ground black pepper

Place a rack in the lower third of your oven and preheat it to 425°F (220°C). Use the convection fan if available.

To prepare the sunchokes, in a mixing bowl, stir together the ingredients. Spread the sunchokes out in a single layer on a baking sheet and roast them until they're golden and crispy, 30–40 minutes. Flip them over at the halfway mark during the roasting process.

To make the māst-o khiār, while the sunchokes roast, stir together the ingredients in a small mixing bowl, then set it aside in the fridge.

When it's time to serve, arrange the roasted sunchokes on a serving platter and generously spread the māst-o khiār over them.

NOTES

Sunchokes' unique shape can trap dirt in crevices, so be sure to wash them well.

You can choose Greek yogurt when making māst-o khiār to create a thicker texture, turning it into a perfect dip.

CAULIFLOWER STEAKS WITH CREAMY TOMATO SAUCE

MAKES 4 SERVINGS • V

It's remarkable how cauliflower has evolved into such a versatile ingredient, even earning the title of "steak"! In this recipe, cauliflower steaks are topped with a creamy, cashew-based tomato sauce infused with a rich blend of spices, creating a perfect vegetarian dish.

FOR THE CAULIFLOWER STEAKS

4 tablespoons (60 ml) olive oil, divided

1 large cauliflower, leaves removed

2 teaspoons apple cider vinegar

1 teaspoon soy sauce

1 clove garlic, finely minced

¼ teaspoon sea salt

¼ teaspoon ground black pepper

¼ teaspoon ground turmeric

To prepare the cauliflower, preheat the oven to 425°F (220°C). Brush a baking sheet with 1 tablespoon of the oil and set aside.

Trim the stem of the cauliflower so that it can sit flat on the cutting board. Slice the cauliflower into ¾-inch (2-cm)-thick steaks by cutting from the top to the bottom. This should yield three or four steaks, depending on the size of the cauliflower. Reserve any leftover pieces for later use, or roast them separately.

Mix 2 tablespoons of the oil with the remaining ingredients in a small bowl. Brush both sides of each cauliflower steak with the marinade, ensuring they are well coated. Transfer the cauliflower steaks to the prepared baking sheet and roast them for 15 minutes. Carefully remove them from the oven, brush them with the remaining 1 tablespoon of olive oil, and flip them over. Roast until they're tender but still have a slight bite, another 10 minutes.

To make the sauce, while the cauliflower is roasting, heat a frying pan over medium heat and add the bay leaves, cardamom, cloves, cinnamon, cumin, and coriander. While cooking, keep stirring the spices with a wooden spatula until they become aromatic, about 90 seconds. Take great care not to burn them. Remove the spices from the pan and set them aside for now.

FOR THE SAUCE

2 bay leaves

2 green cardamom pods

2 whole cloves

1 cinnamon stick

½ teaspoon cumin seeds

½ teaspoon coriander seeds

2 tablespoons ghee

½ red onion, sliced

1 small red chile pepper, or to taste

2 cloves garlic, sliced

½-inch (12-mm) piece of fresh ginger, peeled and sliced

¼ teaspoon ground nutmeg

¼ teaspoon ground turmeric

2 tomatoes, quartered

½ teaspoon sea salt

¼ cup (30 g) raw cashews

½ cup (120 ml) water

2 tablespoons chopped fresh parsley

Add the ghee to the pan and raise the heat to medium-high. Once the ghee has melted, add the onion and sauté for 5 minutes. Return the toasted spices to the pan and add the red chile, garlic, ginger, nutmeg, and turmeric. Keep stirring for another couple of minutes to intensify all of the aromatics. Add the tomatoes, salt, and cashews and keep stirring until the tomatoes have broken down, about 5 minutes. Pour in the water, cover, and cook over low heat for 5 minutes.

Remove the cinnamon stick and bay leaves and transfer the mixture to a blender. Process at high speed until you have a silky smooth texture, about 1 minute. Return the sauce to the frying pan and simmer for 5 minutes to continue building depth into the sauce.

To serve, place the cauliflower steaks on a platter, generously drizzle the sauce over the steaks, and sprinkle with the parsley.

CHAPTER 5

RICE DISHES

Rice with a Crispy Saffron Layer • **VG GF**
Polo bā Tahdig • **95**

Sour Cherry Rice with Petite Meatballs • **GF**
Ālbālu Polo bā Ghel Gheli • **97**

Saffron Carrot Rice with Braised Tofu • **VG GF**
Havij Polo bā Tofu • **101**

Green Bean Rice with Beef • **GF**
Lubiā Polo • **103**

Butternut Squash Rice with Sunny-Side-Up Eggs • **V GF**
Kadu Polo ba Nimru • **107**

Saffron Barberry Rice with Braised Chicken • **GF**
Zereshk Polo bā Morgh • **109**

Cilantro Rice with Chickpeas • **VG GF**
Geshniz Polo ba Nokhod • **112**

Afghan Rice Pilaf with Lamb • **GF**
Ghābeli Palāu • **115**

Spiced Herb Rice with Prawns • **GF**
Meygu Polo • **117**

Herb Rice with Fish • **GF**
Sabzi Polo bā Māhi • **119**

Saffron Risotto • **GF**
Risotto alla Milanese • **122**

V • VEGETARIAN   **VG** • VEGAN   **GF** • GLUTEN FREE

THE OPEN DOOR

BOULDER, CO | 1998

After two long days of driving, I arrived in Boulder in mid-September. The warm, bright Colorado afternoon delighted me as I pulled into the school driveway. The doors were unlocked and wide open.

I was in the midst of making one of the most significant leaps of my life. I had left behind my career in biotech, something that had fulfilled my and my family's expectations since I was a young child in Iran. Despite a responsible role and a good income, I'd become less and less happy in my work, and months of contemplation had led me to a decision: I would transition to food as a second career.

Cooking had always brought me joy. I eagerly watched PBS cooking shows and experimented with recipes at home. I delved deeper into the food world, taking cooking classes at my local co-op and discovering how flavors and techniques represented different cultures. I wanted an intimate and personal connection with food and with people, and could dimly see a potential career as a personal chef.

The School of Natural Cookery in Boulder was the first step. I had swerved out of my predictable path into an intensive course in plant-based, intuitive cooking!

As I made my way into the school, it became clear that it was also a house: a schoolhouse!

There was no one in evidence, but an array of candles, ceremonial bowls, and flowers suggested that some kind of gathering might have taken place recently. I called into the house to announce my arrival, and opted to wait outside on a wooden chair underneath the school logo. This was to become a place of respite on many future occasions.

After a while, I was greeted by a delightful, cheery woman who introduced herself as Julianaa, the school's director and primary teacher. I had spent hours talking to her on the phone before deciding to attend the school, and now I was face to face with this woman who was ultimately going to change my life. She gave me a tour of the school, and I learned that the party remnants were because she had just celebrated her fiftieth birthday.

At thirty-five, I was the oldest student in the class, which comprised eight students. Having failed to secure independent housing in Boulder, I was deemed mature enough to be trusted to be the school's first live-in student. The rules of the schoolhouse were explicit: I was to respect the teacher-student relationship both in and out of class. Simple!

Doubts and fears came rushing in as I unpacked. This school was not what I had pictured, and I started to second-guess my decision to come here. But all I could do was double down on my leap of faith and embrace the change I had started. Little did I know that a transformation had already begun and would occur at a cellular level within me.

> **Without leaps of imagination or dreaming, we lose the excitement of possibilities. Dreaming, after all, is a form of planning.**
>
> —GLORIA STEINEM

The next few months were filled with learning, practicing, exploring, succeeding, and failing. Week after week, we would learn new skills in preparing vegetables, grains, and plant-based proteins. Soups, sauces, baking, and meal planning followed. Days were split between observing Julianaa's cooking process and practicing the methods of the previous day. Just weeks before, I had been overwhelmed by stress and seemingly trapped in my biotech position. Now I was discovering a new way to cook and exploring new methods, all while trusting my intuition in the process. I reveled in this experiential learning style, which was to play a considerable role in my next big life transition when I decided to become a mental health therapist.

Working on sauces provided an unanticipated learning opportunity. Our assignment was to prepare three different styles of sauce. I struggled with one in particular, which consisted of a flavorful liquid, a starch binder, salt, and other seasonings. After multiple attempts to rescue the sauce, which just tasted "off," I gave up and threw the whole thing down the sink.

As always on our cooking days, we gathered around the table and presented our food to Julianaa and our classmates for critique. When it came time for me to serve my sauce, I had to confess my failure to produce one. Perplexed, Julianaa tilted her head and said, very thoughtfully, "Well, that was a cowardly thing to do." Embarrassment, regret, and shame washed over me in a way that required some processing. That tough day ultimately led to one of my most memorable experiences and learnings: It taught me the importance of courage, accountability, and showing up.

I recently told this story to Julianaa, who, after all these years, has become like a second mother to me. She was mortified to be reminded of what she had said on "sauce day," but I assured her that it was some of the best feedback I'd ever received.

RICE AND TAHDIG

RICE IN IRAN

Rice—*berenj* in Persian—is a dietary staple in Iranian cuisine. The northern part of the country, alongside the Caspian Sea, provides a warm, humid, and fertile environment in which rice cultivation thrives.

Known also as *polo* or *chelo* when cooked, rice graces both lunch and dinner spreads. When prepared in its simplest form, rice becomes the essential accompaniment to an assortment of dishes like khoreshes or kukus, often further complemented by yogurt, torshi (pickled vegetables), or sabzi khordan (fresh herbs).

However, Iranian rice dishes range far beyond the simple. Many of them are renowned for their multidimensional taste profiles, featuring a flavorful array of vegetables, meats, herbs, and spices. And then there's texture: Iranian rice dishes feature both a remarkably airy and delicate texture on the inside and a crispy outside layer called *tahdig*. Both of these components are achieved through thoughtfully developed cooking techniques.

The word *tahdig* is a combination of two Persian words. *Tah* means "bottom," while *dig* refers to a pot, so tahdig literally translates to "the bottom of the pot." Cooked on the bottom of the pan, tahdig is typically served on top of the rice by flipping the whole dish over onto a large plate.

Tahdig is not a standalone dish, but rather the most distinctive component of Iranian rice. It introduces a delightful crunch and an extra dimension of taste and mouthfeel.

TIPS FOR COOKING RICE AND TAHDIG

If you haven't made Iranian rice before, I recommend trying the simplest rice and tahdig recipe (see page 95) before moving on to the more complex, layered rice dishes.

Whatever recipe you're following, basmati rice, with its irresistible aroma and unique light texture, is the top variety to use.

Soaking and rinsing play a vital role. The rice must be soaked for at least 1 hour (or up to 5 hours) and then rinsed multiple times with cool water. This process helps eliminate the starches that might otherwise lead to a stickier texture.

Too much oil will make the tahdig greasy and undesirable, while too little will make it unpleasantly crunchy and dry.

When steaming the rice, wrapping the lid with a towel ensures that the moisture is retained in the pot and prevents water from dripping down onto the rice. This is one key factor in cooking Iranian rice to ensure it turns out light and fluffy. Be sure to keep the edges of the towel away from the heat, securing them to the lid handle if you can.

It is essential that you resist the temptation to lift the lid or stir the rice, both of which will interfere with the cooking process.

When you make more complex dishes, you'll layer combinations of meat, vegetables, herbs, and spices into the rice, and then gently mix everything with a fork before cooking.

TAHDIG VARIATIONS

You can create a wonderful, tangy flavor in your tahdig by combining a modest amount of yogurt with the rice and saffron mixture that's spread over the bottom of the pot.

Rice itself is the primary, traditional base for the tahdig, as described above. However, you can also create tahdig with ¼-inch (6-mm)-thick slices of potatoes, lavash bread, or tortillas. Use these ingredients to create the base layer on the bottom of the pot before adding the parboiled rice on top.

This is your chance to have some fun and explore using various spices and vegetables, so feel free to get creative and experiment!

A FINAL WORD

If you're trying Iranian rice and tahdig for the first time, I encourage you to be patient with yourself. Developing a good rhythm and a method for making the rice will come with time. Achieving a perfectly crispy, golden tahdig takes more than following the recipe: It requires practice, patience, and acceptance!

If you find that your first tahdig is slightly less than crispy, or conversely a bit overcooked, think of it as just part of the learning process. Take note of the stove's heat setting during your first try, and make adjustments next time by increasing or decreasing the temperature. You probably won't need to make big adjustments.

Something I always emphasize to my students is that every tahdig behaves differently. Even after years of experience, I still sometimes end up with a tahdig that's extra-crispy or even burnt!

Polo bā Tahdig

RICE WITH A CRISPY SAFFRON LAYER

MAKES 4–6 SERVINGS · VG GF

This recipe is for the classic Iranian rice with a crispy layer that combines contrasting textures with delicious flavors. It's the perfect complement to a wide range of dishes, from hearty stews and braises to grilled meats and vegetables.

Preparing Iranian rice can be a time-consuming process, but trust me when I say that the final creation is worth the effort! With a little practice and patience, you'll be whipping up delicious batches of Iranian rice that your friends and family will absolutely love. So don't be intimidated—give it a try and see for yourself just how delicious this dish can be!

- 8¼ cups (2 l) water, divided
- 2 tablespoons sea salt
- 2 cups (400 g) basmati rice, soaked for at least 1 hour and rinsed
- 5 tablespoons (75 ml) neutral oil, divided
- ½ teaspoon saffron threads, ground and bloomed with 1 tablespoon hot water

To parboil the rice, you will need a large stockpot, much like the pot you would use to boil pasta. Pour in 8 cups (1.9 l) of the water, add the salt, cover the pot, crank up the heat to high, and bring the water to a boil. Once you see steam or hear the lid jiggling, you are ready to add your previously soaked and rinsed rice.

The water must be brought back to a boil after adding the rice, and I recommend doing this without a lid to reduce the risk of the pot boiling over. Leave the heat on high, and keep an eye on it as some foam may form on top; if that happens, turn the heat down just a notch. Continue to boil the rice for 5–7 minutes, depending on the brand. As always, knowing what you are looking for is better than just setting a timer, and what you are looking for is an al dente texture. The rice should be visibly lengthened and look more translucent. But ultimately, your palate is your best tool. Carefully sample a few grains of the rice, which should be softened but still have a bite.

Carefully pour the rice into a colander or fine-mesh strainer, rinse it with cool water, and set it aside to drain.

CONTINUED

NOTES

Don't worry about the hefty amount of salt you use in the parboiling stage. Most of it will be rinsed away, but you'll appreciate having properly salted the rice, bringing out its full flavor.

To make tahdig that won't burn and that you can flip out of the dish, creating a spectacular presentation, you will need a nonstick pot. A 2-quart (1.9 l) pot is about right for 2 cups (400 g) of rice. If you don't have a nonstick pot, you can use a regular one, but don't try to flip it. Also, you will want to wait 5 minutes after cooking before you remove the rice (and then the tahdig) using a spatula.

It's now time to assemble the rice, starting by setting up the tahdig. As you do so, remember that parboiled rice should be handled gently and without excessive stirring, which can break the grains. Add enough oil to create a thin layer across the bottom of your pot, about 3 tablespoons. If you're using a large pot you will need a little more oil. In a small mixing bowl, gently mix 1 cup (135 g) of the parboiled rice with the saffron water and spread evenly over the bottom of the pot. Carefully add the rest of the rice to the pot, and then evenly pour the remaining 2 tablespoons of oil and ¼ cup (60 ml) of water over it.

Wrap the lid with a clean towel and place it securely on the pot. Let the rice steam over medium-low heat for 45 minutes.

Take the lid and the towel it's wrapped in off the pot and place a plate that's at least 2 inches (5 cm) wider than the pot upside down on top of it. Confirm that the handles of the pot are cool enough to touch. Then, hold both handles with your thumbs positioned over the plate. Lift the pot and plate to about chest height, and swiftly, confidently, and carefully turn the pot and plate over. Soften your knees as you slowly lower and slide the pot and plate onto a table or kitchen counter. Finally, slowly raise the pot to unveil the beautifully cooked and fluffy rice wrapped in a crispy, golden tahdig shell.

Congratulations on your dedication and patience in preparing this dish! This humble pot of rice serves as a wonderful connection to the generations of Iranians who have honed the skill of crafting rice.

Ālbālu Polo bā Ghel Gheli

SOUR CHERRY RICE WITH PETITE MEATBALLS

MAKES 4 SERVINGS • GF

Ālbālu is the Persian word for sour cherries, which are highly prized in Iranian cuisine for their distinctive color and intense flavor. Ālbālu polo truly encompasses a wide array of flavors, from sour and sweet to salty, complemented by soft and crispy textures and vibrant, uplifting colors.

FOR THE RICE MIXTURE

3 cups (500 g) fresh sour cherries, pitted

½ cup (100 g) unrefined cane sugar, or to taste

2 tablespoons unsalted butter

1 teaspoon saffron threads, ground and bloomed in 4 tablespoons (60 ml) hot water, divided

8 cups (1.9 l) water

2 tablespoons sea salt

2 cups (400 g) basmati rice, soaked for 1 hour and rinsed

3 tablespoons neutral oil

There are several steps to making Iranian rice dishes, so make sure you have your ingredients and equipment lined up and have given yourself enough time.

To make the rice mixture, place the cherries and sugar in a saucepan, stir, and bring to a gentle simmer over medium heat. Reduce the heat to low, cover, and let the cherries soften as the juices cook down, about 20 minutes. Combined with the sugar, the juice from the cherries will create a luscious cherry syrup that will be used later. You know your syrup is ready when it nicely coats the back of a spoon.

Using a strainer, strain the cherries and reserve the syrup. Return the cherries to the saucepan, add the butter and 3 tablespoons of the saffron water, and mix gently over low heat to melt the butter, a couple of minutes. Remove from the heat and set aside.

Next bring the water and salt to a boil in a large pot. Add the rinsed rice and boil on high heat for 5–7 minutes until it slightly softens. Carefully pour the rice into a colander, rinse it with cool water, and set it aside to drain.

It's now time to assemble the rice, starting by setting up the tahdig. Add the oil to your 2-quart (1.9 l) nonstick pot, creating a thin layer across the bottom. If you're using a large pot, you will need a little more oil. In a small mixing bowl, combine 1 cup (135 g) of the parboiled rice with the remaining 1 tablespoon of saffron water, mix gently, and then spread evenly over the bottom of the pot.

CONTINUED

FOR THE MEATBALLS

1 lb (450 g) ground beef or lamb

1 small onion, grated

1 teaspoon sea salt

½ teaspoon ground black pepper

½ teaspoon ground turmeric

¼ teaspoon ground cinnamon

¼ teaspoon ground cardamom

¼ cup (60 ml) neutral oil

FOR THE GARNISH

1 tablespoon pistachios, coarsely chopped

1 tablespoon slivered almonds

Using a large spatula, layer a third of the remaining parboiled rice and a third of the sour cherries into the pot. Repeat until all of the rice and cherries have been used. Give it a gentle stir to mix everything except the bottom layer, which shouldn't be disturbed.

Wrap the lid with a clean towel and place it securely on the pot. Let the rice steam over medium-low heat for 45 minutes.

To make the meatballs, while the rice is steaming, place all of the ingredients except the oil in a mixing bowl. Be sure to mix everything well so the meat mixture feels and looks like a smooth paste.

Take your time to make each meatball by taking a small amount of the meat paste and rolling it between the palms of your hands. These meatballs are typically quite small, about the size of a hazelnut. If you want to make them bigger, the size of a walnut is fine.

Ideally, you should start to cook the meatballs about 15 minutes before the rice will be ready. Select a large frying pan, heat it over medium heat, add the oil, and sauté the meatballs until they are fully cooked and crispy on the outside, about 10 minutes. Be sure to rotate them while cooking. Next, add the cherry syrup to the pan, stir to coat the meatballs with the syrup, and remove from the heat.

Once the rice has cooked for 45 minutes, remove the lid and place a large plate or platter over the pot. Quickly, confidently, and carefully flip the rice to remove it from the pot. Arrange the meatballs alongside or on top of the rice, and garnish with the pistachios and almonds.

> **NOTES**
>
> *Finding fresh sour cherries can be a challenge, but frozen sour cherries, also known as pie cherries, are widely available and easier to come by. Thaw them before starting the recipe.*

Havij Polo bā Tofu

SAFFRON CARROT RICE WITH BRAISED TOFU

MAKES 4 SERVINGS • VG GF

What sets this dish apart are its simplicity and its mildly sweet, aromatic flavors. Lightly sautéed carrots are combined with fragrant candied orange and tossed with bloomed saffron, resulting in a colorful and vibrant dish that will surely be a visual and gastronomic hit at any gathering.

FOR THE RICE MIXTURE

1 navel orange

½ cup (100 g) unrefined cane sugar

8½ cups (2 l) water, divided

5 tablespoons (75 ml) neutral oil, divided

4 carrots (about ¾ lb/ 360 g total), cut into thin matchsticks

2 tablespoons plus ¼ teaspoon sea salt, divided

1 teaspoon saffron threads, ground and bloomed in 4 tablespoons (60 ml) hot water, divided

2 cups (400 g) basmati rice, soaked for 1 hour and rinsed

To make the rice mixture, using a paring knife, peel the orange, eliminating as much of the pith as possible, before slicing the peel into thin matchsticks. Save the flesh of the orange for another use.

Place the orange peel in a small saucepan with the sugar and ½ cup (120 ml) of the water, give it a good stir, and bring to a simmer. Simmer over medium heat until the syrup has been reduced by half, about 15 minutes. Set aside.

Heat a frying pan over medium heat, then add 2 tablespoons of the oil. Once the oil is heated, add the carrots and sauté them until they are brightened in color and slightly softened, about 5 minutes. Next, add the orange peel and syrup, ¼ teaspoon of the salt, and 3 tablespoons of the saffron water. Mix and cook for 1 minute before turning the heat off. Set aside.

To parboil the rice, begin by bringing the remaining 8 cups (1.9 l) of water and remaining 2 tablespoons of salt to a boil in a large pot. Add the rice and boil over high heat for 5–7 minutes until it slightly softens. Carefully pour the rice into a colander, rinse it with cool water, and set it aside to drain.

It's now time to assemble the rice, starting by setting up the tahdig. Add the remaining 3 tablespoons of oil to your nonstick pot, creating a thin layer across the bottom. If you're using a large pot, you will need a little more oil. In a small mixing bowl, combine 1 cup (135 g) of the parboiled rice with the remaining 1 tablespoon of saffron water, mix gently, and then spread evenly over the bottom of the pot.

CONTINUED

FOR THE TOFU

1 package (1 lb/450 g) extra-firm tofu

4 tablespoons (60 ml) neutral oil, divided

1 small onion, finely diced

2 cloves garlic, minced

½ teaspoon ground turmeric

¼ teaspoon ground cumin

¼ teaspoon ground cinnamon

1 tablespoon tomato paste

1 cup (240 ml) water

2 tablespoons fresh lemon juice

⅔ teaspoon sea salt

¼ teaspoon ground black pepper

FOR THE GARNISH

2 tablespoons pistachios, coarsely chopped

NOTES

It's worth acknowledging that while tofu or sunny-side-up eggs are my preferred proteins for this dish, havij polo is traditionally served with braised beef, lamb, or chicken.

Orange marmalade is a good substitute for the candied orange in this recipe. Depending on your taste, 2 to 3 tablespoons of marmalade should suffice.

Using a large spatula, layer a third of the parboiled rice and a third of the carrot and orange mixture into the pot. Repeat until all of the rice and carrot mixture have been used. Give it a gentle stir to mix everything except the bottom layer, which shouldn't be disturbed.

Wrap the lid with a clean towel and place it securely on the pot. Let the rice steam over medium-low heat for 45 minutes.

Prepare the tofu while the rice is cooking, about 30 minutes before you are ready to serve everything. Slice the tofu into ½-inch (12-mm)-thick slabs and pat them dry with paper towels.

Heat a large frying pan over medium-high heat, then add 2 tablespoons of the oil. Once the oil is visibly hot and spreads across the surface, carefully add the tofu pieces. Sauté on both sides until you observe some crispiness and color, about 4 minutes on each side. Remove the tofu from the pan and set aside.

Reduce the heat to medium, add the remaining 2 tablespoons of oil, and sauté the onion until lightly golden, about 10 minutes. Add the garlic, turmeric, cumin, and cinnamon and sauté for 2 more minutes. Stir in the tomato paste and sauté for another 2 minutes to bring out the tomato flavor.

Finally, add the water, lemon juice, salt, and pepper and stir before placing the tofu in the sauce. Cover and simmer over low heat for 30 minutes to allow the tofu to absorb the flavors of the sauce. Taste everything and adjust the seasonings if necessary.

When the rice is done, remove the lid and put a large plate or platter over the pot. Flip the rice quickly, confidently, and carefully to remove it from the pot.

You can present the braised tofu on a separate serving dish or arrange it around the rice. Sprinkle the pistachios over the tofu.

Grab a spatula and break through the crispy crust to reveal the vibrant and aromatic gems hidden beneath the golden tahdig layer.

Lubiā Polo

GREEN BEAN RICE WITH BEEF

MAKES 4–6 SERVINGS • GF

My aunt, Ameh Āzar, possessed a unique culinary talent, and to this day I have yet to encounter a lubiā polo that matches hers. Her not-so-secret ingredient was the aromatic and flavorful roghan kermānshāhi, a type of sheep or beef ghee originating from the city of Kermanshah in western Iran.

It never fails to astonish me how a familiar taste or aroma can evoke myriad emotions. This dish is a tribute to Ameh Āzar's remarkable skills and enduring memory.

FOR THE BEEF AND GREEN BEANS

4 tablespoons (60 g) ghee, divided

1 onion, diced

1 teaspoon ground turmeric

4 cups (600 g) green beans, trimmed and cut into ½-inch (12-mm) pieces

1 lb (450 g) beef chuck or round, cut into ½-inch (12-mm) cubes

1½ teaspoons sea salt

1 teaspoon ground black pepper

1 teaspoon ground cinnamon

6 tablespoons (90 g) tomato paste

¼ cup (60 ml) fresh lemon juice

½ cup (120 ml) water

To prepare the beef and green beans, heat a large frying pan over medium heat, add 2 tablespoons of the ghee, and wait for it to melt. Sauté the onion until it becomes translucent, 5–7 minutes.

Sprinkle in the turmeric and sauté for a couple more minutes before adding the green beans. Continue sautéing the green beans over medium heat to bring out their flavors and brighten them up, about 5 minutes. Transfer everything from the pan to a bowl.

Add the remaining 2 tablespoons of ghee to the same pan and sauté the beef over high heat until lightly browned, about 5 minutes. Reduce the heat to low, cover, and let the beef cook in its own juices for 15 minutes.

Return the onion and green bean mixture to the pan. Add the salt, pepper, cinnamon, and tomato paste and stir. Cook for 2 minutes over medium heat to deepen their flavors.

Pour in the lemon juice and water. Cover the pan and let it cook over low heat until the green beans and meat have softened, about 30 minutes. Adjust the water as needed, but remember the stew should be thick in consistency and not watery. The stew will be quite bold and with strong flavors at this stage, which will mellow out when mixed with the rice.

CONTINUED

FOR THE RICE

8 cups (1.9 l) water

2 tablespoons sea salt

2 cups (400 g) basmati rice, soaked for at least 1 hour and rinsed

3 tablespoons ghee, melted

1 small russet potato, peeled and cut into ¼-inch (6-mm)-thick rounds

To prepare the rice, while the stew is cooking, bring the water and the salt to a boil in a large pot. Add the rice and boil over high heat for 5–7 minutes until it slightly softens. Carefully pour the rice into a colander, rinse it with cool water, and set it aside to drain.

It's now time to assemble the rice, starting by setting up the tahdig. Add the melted ghee to your nonstick pot, creating a thin layer across the bottom. If you're using a large pot, you will need a little more ghee. Fan the potatoes over the bottom, overlapping them. This will become the crispy potato tahdig.

Using a large spatula, layer a third of the parboiled rice and a third of the beef and green bean mixture in the pot. Repeat until all of the rice and beef and green bean mixture have been used. Give it a gentle stir to mix everything except the bottom layer, which shouldn't be disturbed.

Wrap the lid with a clean towel and place it securely on the pot. Let the rice steam over medium-low heat for 45 minutes.

To serve, select a large plate or platter to place on top of the pan and flip the rice quickly, confidently, and carefully to remove it from the pot.

Pair this with a side of yogurt or pickled vegetables. You may also enjoy a dab of ghee on top of your rice to make it extra special, just like I did when eating this at my Ameh Āzar's house.

Kadu Polo ba Nimru

BUTTERNUT SQUASH RICE WITH SUNNY-SIDE-UP EGGS

MAKES 4 SERVINGS • **V GF**

This dish exemplifies northern Iranian cuisine, embracing simplicity and highlighting the use of fresh, locally sourced eggs to create a satisfying meal. Kadu polo is a flavorful yet uncomplicated dish, making it the ideal comfort food for the fall season.

FOR THE BUTTERNUT SQUASH

¼ cup (60 ml) olive oil

1 large onion, thinly sliced

2 cups (280 g) diced butternut squash

1 teaspoon sea salt

1 teaspoon ground turmeric

¼ teaspoon ground cinnamon

2-4 tablespoons (25-50 g) unrefined cane sugar, to taste

FOR THE RICE

8 cups (1.9 l) water

2 tablespoons sea salt

2 cups (400 g) basmati rice, soaked for 1 hour and rinsed

3 tablespoons neutral oil

½ teaspoon ground turmeric mixed with 2 tablespoons water

FOR THE EGGS

2 tablespoons unsalted butter

4 eggs

¼ teaspoon sea salt

¼ teaspoon ground black pepper

To prepare the butternut squash, select a large frying pan and place it on the stove over medium heat until nice and warm, then add the olive oil.

Add the onion to the pan and cook until it becomes lightly golden, about 10 minutes. Toss in the butternut squash and keep sautéing for another 5 minutes.

Add the salt, turmeric, and cinnamon and stir to ensure the spices coat the squash. Sauté for another minute. Taste the squash and, depending on the sweetness level, add 2-4 tablespoons (25-50 g) of sugar. Sprinkle in the sugar and stir to mix. Remove the pan from the heat and set it aside.

To prepare the rice, start by bringing the water and salt to a boil in a large pot. Add the rice and boil over high heat for 5-7 minutes until it slightly softens. Carefully pour the rice into a colander, rinse it with cool water, and set it aside to drain.

It's now time to assemble the rice, starting by setting up the tahdig. Add the oil to your nonstick pot, creating a thin layer across the bottom. If you're using a large pot, you will need a little more oil. In a small mixing bowl, combine 1 cup (135 g) of the parboiled rice with the turmeric and water, mix gently, and then spread evenly over the bottom of the pot.

CONTINUED

RICE DISHES | 107

Using a large spatula, layer a third of the remaining parboiled rice and a third of the squash mixture in the pot. Repeat until all of the rice and butternut squash have been used. Give it a gentle stir to mix everything except the bottom layer, which shouldn't be disturbed.

Wrap the lid with a clean towel and place it securely on the pot. Let the rice steam over medium-low heat for 45 minutes.

To make the eggs, heat a frying pan for a few minutes over medium heat. Once heated, add the butter and tilt the pan to help it spread and melt. Crack the eggs into the pan, sprinkle with the salt and pepper, and partially cover. Cook for 2–3 minutes for sunny-side-up eggs or longer, depending on your preference.

To serve the rice, choose a large plate or platter and place it on top of the pan. Then, flip the rice quickly, confidently, and carefully to remove it from the pot.

Grab a spatula and break through the crispy crust to reveal the golden rice and tender squash beneath the crispy tahdig layer. Serve with sunny-side-up eggs.

> **NOTES**
>
> *To enhance both the flavor and the texture, consider garnishing the dish with crispy fried shallots (see page 42) and walnut pieces.*

Zereshk Polo bā Morgh

SAFFRON BARBERRY RICE WITH BRAISED CHICKEN

MAKES 4 SERVINGS • **GF**

At the heart of zereshk polo lie the barberries, vibrant and tangy, their bright colors adding a visual feast to the dish. These tart berries are balanced by butter and sugar, and a glistening touch of saffron adds opulence. The barberries are generously layered within fluffy rice, and the whole is topped with succulent chicken to create a sensual feast.

FOR THE CHICKEN

2 tablespoons olive oil

4 chicken thighs (about 1½ lb/680 g total), bone in and skin on

1 onion, diced

1 teaspoon ground turmeric

2 tablespoons tomato paste

⅔ cup (160 ml) water

1 teaspoon sea salt

½ teaspoon ground black pepper

2 teaspoons saffron threads, ground and bloomed with 6 tablespoons (90 ml) hot water, divided

FOR THE RICE

8¼ cups (2 l) water, divided

2 tablespoons sea salt

2 cups (400 g) basmati rice, soaked for 1 hour and rinsed

5 tablespoons (75 ml) neutral oil, divided

1 tablespoon saffron water, from above

To prepare the chicken, heat a large frying pan over medium-high heat and add the oil. Once the oil is hot and evenly coats the surface, carefully place the chicken pieces in the pan, skin side down. Sauté them to develop some crispiness and color, about 5 minutes on each side. Remove the chicken from the pan for now.

Reduce the heat to medium and sauté the onion in the same pan until lightly golden, about 10 minutes. Sprinkle in the turmeric and stir for 2 minutes before adding the tomato paste. Continue stirring for another 2 minutes to enhance the tomato flavor. Add the water, salt, and pepper and stir to combine.

Return the chicken pieces to the pan, cover, and cook over low heat for 70–75 minutes.

To prepare the rice, while the chicken is cooking, bring 8 cups (1.9 l) of the water and the salt to a boil in a large pot. Add the rice and boil over high heat for 5–7 minutes until it slightly softens. Carefully pour the rice into a colander, rinse it with cool water, and set it aside to drain.

CONTINUED

RICE DISHES | 109

FOR THE BARBERRIES

2 tablespoons unsalted butter

²⁄₃ cup (40 g) dried barberries, rinsed

2-4 tablespoons (25-50 g) sugar, to taste

3 tablespoons saffron water, from page 109

FOR THE GARNISH

1 tablespoon pistachios, coarsely chopped

NOTES

Braised lamb or beef is a suitable alternative to chicken. I love zereshk polo with roasted seasoned tofu.

It's now time to assemble the rice, starting by setting up the tahdig. Add 3 tablespoons of the oil to your nonstick pot, creating a thin layer across the bottom. If you're using a large pot, you will need a little more oil. In a small mixing bowl, combine 1 cup (135 g) of the parboiled rice with 1 tablespoon of the saffron water, mix gently, and then spread evenly over the bottom of the pot.

Gently add the remainder of the rice to the pot. Evenly drizzle the remaining 2 tablespoons of oil and remaining ¼ cup (60 ml) of water over the top of the rice.

Wrap the lid with a clean towel and place it securely on the pot. Let the rice steam over medium-low heat for 45 minutes.

About 5 minutes before the rice is ready, add 2 tablespoons of the saffron water to the chicken, stir, and remove from the heat. The chicken should be fork-tender at this stage.

To prepare the barberries, gently melt the butter in a small saucepan and add the barberries, sugar, and remaining 3 tablespoons of saffron water to the pan. Stir everything over low heat until the sugar dissolves and the barberries become lively and bright. Be careful not to burn the berries during this process, which should take no more than 2-4 minutes.

Using a large spatula, gently remove the fluffy rice from the pot and transfer it onto a serving platter. Carefully remove the tahdig in large pieces and arrange them alongside the rice.

Drizzle the barberry mixture over the rice and lightly fluff it with a fork to evenly distribute the barberries.

Arrange the chicken pieces around the rice and sprinkle the pistachios on top.

Geshniz Polo ba Nokhod

CILANTRO RICE WITH CHICKPEAS

MAKES 4 SERVINGS • **VG GF**

Here's another dish featuring an abundance of herbs. While sabzi polo incorporates a variety of herbs, others, like geshniz polo, focus on just one—in this case, cilantro. Combined with a flavorful spiced chickpea stew, it creates a delicious and satisfying vegan meal.

FOR THE RICE

8¼ cups (2 l) water, divided

2 tablespoons sea salt

2 cups (400 g) basmati rice, soaked for 1 hour and rinsed

½ cup (10 g) dried cilantro

5 tablespoons (75 ml) neutral oil, divided

To prepare the rice, bring 8 cups (1.9 l) of the water and the salt to a boil in a large pot. Add the rice and boil over high heat for 5–7 minutes until it softens slightly. Add the dried cilantro and give everything a gentle but thorough stir. Drain the rice mixture in a fine-mesh strainer and rinse with cool water.

Choose a pot with a nonstick surface, add 3 tablespoons of the neutral oil and spread it around evenly on the bottom of the pot, and then transfer the rice and cilantro mixture on top.

Evenly pour the remaining ¼ cup (60 ml) of water and remaining 2 tablespoons of oil over the top of the rice, lightly fluffing it with a fork.

Wrap the pot lid with a clean towel and place it on top of the pot. Let the rice steam over medium-low heat for 45 minutes.

To make the chickpea stew, while the rice is cooking, toast the cumin, coriander, and mustard seeds in a large frying pan over medium heat until they become aromatic, 1–2 minutes. Let the spices cool, and then grind them into a powder using a mortar and pestle or spice grinder. Set aside.

FOR THE CHICKPEA STEW

½ teaspoon cumin seeds

¼ teaspoon coriander seeds

¼ teaspoon yellow mustard seeds

2 tablespoons olive oil

1 onion, diced

2 cloves garlic, minced

½ teaspoon ground turmeric

1 small red chile pepper, thinly sliced, or to taste

1 tablespoon tomato paste

1½ cups (250 g) cooked chickpeas or 1 can (15 oz/425 g) chickpeas, rinsed and drained

⅔ cup (160 ml) water, or as needed

1 bay leaf

1 tablespoon fresh lime juice

½ teaspoon sea salt

¼ cup (8 g) coarsely chopped fresh cilantro

Heat the pan again over medium heat, add the olive oil, and sauté the onion until it turns lightly golden, about 10 minutes. Add the garlic, turmeric, chile pepper, and tomato paste to the pan, sautéing for another 2 minutes to draw out and enhance their flavors.

Now add the chickpeas, water, bay leaf, lime juice, salt, and toasted spices. Cover and simmer over low heat for 20 minutes. Taste and adjust the seasoning while also checking the stew's consistency—it should be dense with ingredients and only a small amount of liquid.

Once the stew has finished cooking, remove the bay leaf and transfer the stew to a serving bowl. Garnish it with the fresh cilantro.

To serve the rice, place a larger plate or platter upside down over the pan. Swiftly invert the rice onto the platter and present it alongside the chickpea stew.

> **NOTES**
> *You can substitute 1½ cups (45 g) of fresh cilantro, coarsely chopped, for the dried cilantro.*

Ghābeli Palāu

AFGHAN RICE PILAF WITH LAMB

MAKES 4 SERVINGS • GF

In 2021, many Afghans were displaced from their native land, and numerous communities came together to support these refugees and asylees. During this time, I had the privilege of partnering with a kindred spirit, Nasrin Noori, a talented Seattle-based Afghan chef and restaurateur.

Our joint efforts culminated in an online event to raise awareness and generate vital funds for Afghan refugees who had recently arrived in the United States. We highlighted Afghanistan's rich culinary heritage by preparing this treasured rice and lamb dish.

I've made minor adjustments to Nasrin's original recipe.

FOR THE AFGHAN CHAR MASALA

1 cinnamon stick

2 brown cardamom pods

2 teaspoons green cardamom pods

2 teaspoons cumin seeds

2 teaspoons coriander seeds

½ teaspoon black peppercorns

¼ teaspoon whole cloves

FOR THE LAMB

1 large onion, quartered

5 cloves garlic

2 tomatoes, quartered

1 tablespoon sea salt

1 teaspoon ground black pepper

1 tablespoon paprika

1 tablespoon ground coriander

1½ cups (360 ml) water, or as needed

2 lamb shanks (about 3 lb/1.4 kg total)

To make the char masala, in a small pan, toast all of the spices over low heat until their aroma is released, 2–3 minutes. Keep an eye on the spices and shake them frequently to avoid over-browning. Let the mixture cool before grinding it into powder in a spice grinder or a sturdy mortar and pestle. Set aside for now.

Preheat the oven to 350°F (180°C).

To prepare the lamb, place all the ingredients except the lamb in a food processor and blend until you have a sauce-like consistency.

Place the lamb in a Dutch oven or an oven-safe dish and pour the sauce over the top, making sure it coats the meat.

Once that's done, cover the dish and place it in the oven. Braise the lamb shanks until the internal temperature has reached 160°F (71°C), about 3 hours. Make sure to rotate the shanks halfway through cooking. Also, check the liquid level simultaneously, adding more water if needed to keep the lamb moist. This slow-cooking process cooks the meat thoroughly and leaves it wonderfully tender.

To make the caramelized sugar, heat the oil in a small saucepan over medium heat. Once the oil is heated, add the sugar. Reduce the heat to low and whisk continuously until the sugar has melted and begun to caramelize, about 5 minutes.

CONTINUED

FOR THE CARAMELIZED SUGAR

¼ cup (60 ml) neutral oil

1 tablespoon sugar

1 cup (240 ml) water

2 teaspoons Afghan char masala, from page 115

½ teaspoon sea salt

FOR THE RICE

8 cups (1.9 l) water

2 tablespoons sea salt

2 cups (400 g) basmati rice, soaked for 1 hour and rinsed

¼ cup (60 ml) neutral oil

FOR THE CARROTS

2 tablespoons neutral oil

4 carrots (about ¾ lb/ 340 g total), cut into thin matchsticks

½ teaspoon ground cardamom

½ cup (85 g) raisins

½ cup (60 g) dried cranberries

¼ cup (50 g) sugar, or to taste

½ cup (60 g) slivered almonds

½ cup (60 g) pistachios, coarsely chopped

Zest of 1 orange

Remove from the heat and let it cool for a minute before adding the water. Return the pan to medium heat and simmer until the sugar is well integrated and the liquid turns a light brown color, about a minute.

Sprinkle in the char masala and salt and give it a good stir before removing the pan from the heat. Set it aside.

To prepare the rice, select a large oven-safe pot and bring the water and salt to a boil. Once boiling, add the rice and bring it back to a boil over high heat. Keep boiling until the rice has slightly softened, 5–7 minutes. Strain the rice into a colander, rinse it with cool water, and let it drain thoroughly.

Return the rice to the pot and drizzle the sugar mixture and oil over the rice. Gently mix until the rice is evenly coated. Cover the pot, place it in the oven, and cook for 35–40 minutes.

To prepare the carrots, while the rice is cooking, heat a frying pan over medium heat, add the oil, and sauté the carrots until they are slightly softened, 6–8 minutes.

Add the cardamom, raisins, cranberries, sugar, almonds, pistachios, and orange zest to the pan and sauté for a couple of minutes. Cover the pan, take it off the heat, and set it aside.

To serve, arrange half of the prepared rice on a large platter, then place the lamb shanks on top. Next, cover the lamb with the remaining rice. Garnish the rice and lamb with the carrot mixture, and serve it while still hot.

NOTES

Brown cardamom pods are typically found in West Asian and Indian markets. If unavailable, there is no perfect substitute, but you can add an extra ¼ teaspoon each of cumin and green cardamom.

The lamb can be cooked in a pressure cooker or an Instant Pot. In this case, cook the lamb for about 45 minutes until fully cooked and tender.

The rice can be cooked on your stovetop instead of in the oven. Cook it over medium-low heat for 35–40 minutes.

Meygu Polo

SPICED HERB RICE WITH PRAWNS

MAKES 4 SERVINGS · GF

Prawns are a staple of Iran's southern provinces, located along the Persian Gulf. Meygu polo, a prominent southern dish, combines prawns with warming spices and fresh herbs, all layered into fluffy rice.

FOR THE HERBS

¼ cup (60 ml) neutral oil

1 onion, thinly sliced

4 cloves garlic, minced

1 teaspoon ground turmeric

1 tablespoon cumin seeds

2 cups (60 g) coarsely chopped fresh dill

2 cups (60 g) coarsely chopped fresh cilantro

1 tablespoon dried fenugreek leaves

FOR THE RICE

8 cups (1.9 l) water

2 tablespoons sea salt

2 cups (400 g) basmati rice, soaked for 1 hour and rinsed

3 tablespoons neutral oil

To prepare the herbs, start by heating a frying pan. Drizzle in the oil and sauté the onion over medium heat until it turns a light golden color, about 10 minutes.

Add the garlic, turmeric, and cumin and continue sautéing for an additional 2 minutes. Stir in the dill, cilantro, and fenugreek and sauté for a couple of minutes. Remove from the heat and set aside.

To prepare the rice, bring the water and salt to a boil in a large pot. Add the rice and boil over high heat for 5–7 minutes until it slightly softens. Carefully pour the rice into a colander and give it a quick rinse with cool water. After draining thoroughly, return the rice to the pot. Gently stir the herb mixture into the rice, creating a uniform blend without overmixing.

Add the oil to your 2-quart (1.9 l) nonstick pot, creating a thin layer across the bottom. If you're using a large pot, you will need a little more oil. Now add all of the rice and herb mixture.

Wrap the lid with a clean towel and place it securely on the pot. Let the rice steam over medium-low heat for 45 minutes.

To prepare the prawns, 10 minutes before the rice is done cooking, place them in a mixing bowl and add all of the spices and salt. Give the prawns a good toss to make sure they're fully coated.

CONTINUED

FOR THE PRAWNS

1½ lb (680 g) uncooked prawns, shelled and deveined

½ teaspoon paprika

¼ teaspoon ground cumin

¼ teaspoon garlic powder

¼ teaspoon chipotle pepper powder, or to taste

½ teaspoon sea salt

2 tablespoons neutral oil

Juice of 1 lime

FOR THE GARNISH

2 tablespoons roughly chopped fresh cilantro

1 lime, cut into wedges

Heat a large frying pan over medium-high heat. Add the oil, then gently lay the prawns in the pan, sautéing until they turn a light pink color, 1–2 minutes on each side. Splash the prawns with the lime juice and remove from the pan.

Using a spatula, gently remove the rice from the pot and transfer to a serving platter. Then, carefully remove the tahdig in large pieces and arrange them alongside the rice.

Place the prawns on top of the rice and garnish with the cilantro and lime wedges.

NOTES

You can get creative with meygu polo. Feel free to increase the spices, cut down on the herbs, add tamarind for tang, or use date molasses for sweetness. Top it off with raisins, pistachios, or almonds.

Sabzi Polo bā Māhi

HERB RICE WITH FISH

MAKES 4 SERVINGS • **GF**

Iranians have a strong fondness for both fresh and dried herbs, creatively integrated into all kinds of dishes, often in surprisingly large quantities. Sabzi polo, notably associated with Nowruz, the Iranian New Year, embodies this affinity.

FOR THE RICE

8¼ cups (2 l) water, divided

2 tablespoons sea salt

2 cups (400 g) basmati rice, soaked for 1 hour and rinsed

1½ cups (45 g) coarsely chopped fresh dill

1 cup (30 g) coarsely chopped fresh parsley

1 cup (30 g) coarsely chopped fresh cilantro

½ cup (45 g) coarsely chopped nira (garlic chives)

5 tablespoons (75 ml) neutral oil, divided

1 teaspoon saffron threads, ground and bloomed with 4 tablespoons (60 ml) hot water, divided

1 tablespoon dried fenugreek leaves

To prepare the rice, bring 8 cups (1.9 l) of the water and the salt to a boil in a large pot. Add the rice and boil over high heat for 5–7 minutes until it slightly softens.

Turn off the heat, and with a slotted spoon, remove 1 cup (135 g) of the parboiled rice, drain, and place in a small mixing bowl. Set it aside.

Toss the herbs into the big pot with the remaining rice and give it a stir to make sure they're all mixed in nicely. Pour this rice and herb mixture into a fine-mesh strainer, rinse with cool water, and set it aside to drain.

It's now time to assemble the rice, starting by setting up the tahdig. Add 3 tablespoons of the oil to your nonstick pot, creating a thin layer across the bottom. If you're using a large pot, you will need a little more oil. Add 1 tablespoon of the saffron water to the small mixing bowl with the 1 cup (135 g) of plain rice, give it a gentle stir, and evenly spread it across the bottom of the pot.

Using a large spatula, add the rice and herb mixture on top. Pour in the remaining ¼ cup (60 ml) of water, remaining 2 tablespoons of oil, and 1 tablespoon of saffron water over the top of the rice, lightly fluffing it with a fork, making sure you don't disturb the bottom layer.

Wrap the lid with a clean towel and place it securely on the pot. Let the rice steam over medium-low heat for 45 minutes.

CONTINUED

FOR THE FISH

2 whole branzino (about 2 lb/900 g total)

1 teaspoon sea salt

½ teaspoon ground black pepper

2 tablespoons saffron water, from page 119

3 tablespoons neutral oil

To prepare the fish, about 20 minutes before the rice is ready, rinse the fish under cool water and pat it dry with paper towels. Season the fish, including the cavity, with the salt and pepper. Using a small brush, apply the remaining 2 tablespoons of saffron water to the exterior of the fish.

Select a frying pan large enough to accommodate the fish, heat it over medium-high heat, and add the oil. Fry the fish for 5–6 minutes on each side, adjusting the cooking time based on the fish's size. The fish will develop a crispy, golden exterior while remaining tender inside.

For serving, place a large plate or platter upside down over the rice pot and quickly invert the rice onto the platter. Transfer the fish to a serving platter and serve with pickled garlic, Seville orange, or lemon wedges.

> **NOTES**
>
> *You can choose from many types of white-fleshed fish, like sea bass, trout, or sea bream. Salmon can also be an excellent substitute. I've presented whole fish in this recipe, but you can opt for smaller filets for simpler preparation and convenience.*
>
> *Regular chives can be used instead of nira (garlic chives) if you prefer.*

Risotto alla Milanese

SAFFRON RISOTTO

MAKES 4 SERVINGS • GF

Chef José Andrés is a hero of mine, both as a chef and as a humanitarian, and I love his exhortation to "build longer tables instead of higher walls." Inspired by him, my Italian friend Paola Albanesi and I teamed up in December 2022 for an online cooking demonstration. Our goals were to increase awareness of the Woman, Life, Freedom movement in Iran and to raise funds to support underprivileged Iranian children.

Food reminds us that nations often have more in common than what divides them. A great example is the similarity of the rice dishes of Italy and Iran. While I prepared an Iranian rice pilaf, Paola demonstrated risotto alla Milanese, a classic risotto made with Carnaroli rice and saffron.

I've made just a few minor adjustments to Paola's original recipe.

5 cups (1.2 l) chicken or vegetable broth, plus more as needed

3 tablespoons unsalted butter, divided

1 shallot, finely minced

2 cups (400 g) Carnaroli or arborio rice

½ teaspoon sea salt

½ cup (120 ml) white wine

¼ teaspoon saffron threads

½ cup (60 g) freshly grated Parmigiano-Reggiano cheese, plus more for garnish

In a 2-quart (1.9 l) saucepan, bring the broth to a gentle simmer and keep it warm during the entire cooking process.

Heat a frying pan over medium-low heat, melt 1 tablespoon of the butter, and add the shallot. Sauté until it becomes translucent, 2–3 minutes.

Add the rice and stir until it becomes lightly toasted and fragrant, 1–2 minutes. Next, add the salt and wine, stirring until the wine is absorbed.

Pour 2 cups (480 ml) of the warm broth into the rice, stir, and keep the heat on medium-low to maintain a simmer. Partially cover the frying pan with a lid and set a timer for 5 minutes. As the rice cooks, give it a quick stir to make sure it's not sticking to the bottom. Add more broth if you notice it getting dry.

As the risotto cooks, grind the saffron threads with a mortar and pestle, then mix the saffron with a ladleful of warm broth in a small mixing bowl.

Once the first 5 minutes have passed and the broth has been partially absorbed, add the saffron broth and stir. Continue to cook, adding broth by the ladleful whenever the rice looks dry, stirring the rice as you do so.

After the rice has cooked for about 15 minutes, you should check and adjust the seasoning. At the same time, start to check the rice for doneness, which typically takes 15–20 minutes. You are looking for the rice to be tender to the bite but still retain a firm texture and not be overly starchy. Strive for a wavy consistency known as "all'onda"; the risotto should flow like a wave of hot lava when you tilt the pot. If needed, add a bit more broth to achieve this texture.

For the final step, crucial for developing the desired creaminess, remove the pot from the heat and add the remaining 2 tablespoons of butter and the cheese. Cover the risotto with a lid and let it rest for 1 minute. Vigorously stir the risotto until the butter and cheese have blended into the remaining liquid and the risotto has a creamy texture, about 15 seconds.

Serve the risotto promptly, garnished with a touch more cheese.

CHAPTER 6

KHORESHES

Chicken in Pomegranate Walnut Sauce • **GF**
Khoresh Fesenjun • **131**

Beef and Herb Stew • **GF**
Khoresh Ghormeh Sabzi • **133**

Beef and Herb Stew with Rhubarb • **GF**
Khoresh Rivās • **136**

Fava Beans with Poached Eggs and Crispy Shallots • **V GF**
Baghāli Ghātogh • **139**

Spinach and Herbs with Poached Eggs • **V GF**
Nargesi • **141**

Beef Stew with Poached Eggs • **GF**
Khoresh Bij Bij • **143**

Chicken Stew with Roasted Peppers and Prunes • **GF**
Jody's Mediterranean Chicken • **145**

Peach and Saffron Chicken Stew • **GF**
Khoresh Hulu • **149**

Petite Meatballs with Crispy Potatoes • **GF**
Khoresh Kalleh Gonjeshki • **151**

Eggplant with Herbs and Poached Eggs • **V GF**
Melā Ghormeh • **155**

Beef and Yellow Split Pea Stew with Crispy Potatoes • **GF**
Khoresh Gheymeh • **156**

Chicken in Tangy Walnut and Herb Sauce • **GF**
Khoresh Morgh Torsh • **159**

Eggplant and Tomato Stew with Sour Grapes • **VG GF**
Khoresh Gojeh Bādemjān • **161**

V • VEGETARIAN   **VG** • VEGAN   **GF** • GLUTEN FREE

EMBRACING THE APRON

SEATTLE, WA | 1998

After graduating from cooking school, I returned to Seattle with a wealth of knowledge and a range of experiences geared toward achieving my goal of becoming a personal chef. However, I couldn't escape the reality that the economic privilege I had enjoyed in my biotech job was now beyond my reach. I was quite unsure of how everything would unfold, but I was certain of my determination to make it work.

To support myself while starting my personal chef venture, I took a job at a bakery. The early January mornings were grueling, waking up at 3 a.m. in the cold darkness of a Seattle winter. My responsibility was to get the shop ready for the day. This included baking premade frozen cookie, scone, and muffin dough and arranging the pastries in the bakery window. Well, no matter how hard I tried, my muffins couldn't seem to agree on a consistent size. After three months, that's why I ended up getting the boot!

Despite the initial dismay of being let go, this experience became the catalyst that pushed me to step up my game and fully dedicate myself to my ultimate goal: creating my own personal chef business. Even to this day, whenever I teach a baking class, I always encourage my students to embrace their individuality and infuse their creations with a touch of rebellion, resulting in uniquely spirited baked goods!

In 1998, personal chefs were a rarity, and online marketing was not as advanced as it is today. But armed with new determination, I told everyone I knew about my new career path. That's when Jody, a former colleague from my biotech days, became my first client.

My first cooking session for Jody feels like it happened just yesterday. I had consulted her in detail about her dietary requirements, allergies, likes, and dislikes. Excited to make a great impression on my inaugural day as a personal chef, I crafted a customized menu and procured fresh groceries from the local co-op before arriving at Jody's home. During a marathon cooking session, I filled her fridge to the brim. As it was my first time cooking on such a scale, I was utterly exhausted by the time I left.

Much to my delight, Jody's review of my dishes was overwhelmingly positive. However, she did have one valuable piece of feedback: I had prepared enough food to feed an army! It seemed that my inclination to make an abundance of food for others was part of my Iranian DNA. Going forward, I adjusted my quantities, but to this day I still struggle not to overfeed my friends and family.

> **Set your life on fire. Seek those who fan your flames.**
>
> —RUMI

Jody became my most devoted supporter, and thanks to her, I acquired more clients from among her colleagues. My carefully crafted meals, filled with love and intentionality, made their way into staff lounges and sparked conversations. Satisfied clients recommended me to friends and family, and I began to build a loyal clientele. The anxiety that had accompanied my career change soon faded away, and I found myself embracing one of the happiest chapters of my life, filled with a sense of freedom, joy, and empowerment.

Within two years of leaving culinary school, I was well established as a personal chef, serving ten families a week. I had also become an instructor, teaching several classes each month on plant-based cuisine and culinary skills. My days were flexible, and I enjoyed the freedom to pursue activities that fulfilled me, particularly those centered on food. To prepare around sixty dishes each week, I delved into food magazines and scoured cookbooks for inspiration. I significantly expanded my knowledge of food, honed my cooking skills, and developed a deeper appreciation for diverse global cuisines.

I cooked for Jody for more than a decade, and later taught her how to cook for herself. If I had set my life on fire, Jody truly was one of those who fanned the flames.

KHORESH

Iran is famous for its stews, or *khoreshes* in Persian. There are many classic khoreshes from all over the country, some of which I've included here, but you can always substitute your own proteins and other ingredients. Once you've learned the principles, I encourage you to experiment to meet your own tastes and preferences.

The principles are important because khoresh has certain characteristics that are simply not optional. Proteins must be fork-tender—Iranians eat stews with a fork and spoon, not a knife—and the consistency of the broth is critical. There's a Persian adjective—*jā oftādeh*, meaning "fallen into place"—for most dishes, but particularly stews, that have been cooked correctly over a gentle heat and allowed to rest before serving. In a khoresh that's jā oftādeh, all of the ingredients have melded together, and the oil has separated and risen to the top. The quality of a stew is often judged by the amount of oil surfacing, which serves as a testament to the richness of the dish.

Most recipes start by sautéing onions with turmeric, creating a fragrant golden base. As a time-saving measure, I sauté onions in large batches, season them with turmeric, and refrigerate them for use throughout the week, effectively shaving off about 20 minutes from the stew-making process.

The primary sources of protein in stews are beef, lamb, chicken, eggs, and beans. Many stews can be prepared with different types of meat to suit your tastes and preferences. When swapping meats, be sure to adjust the cooking time and liquid to cook the meat properly.

Beef chuck or round roasts work particularly well, as do cuts of lamb shoulder, leg, or shank. When using chicken, I like to buy a whole bird, carve it into pieces myself, and use the leftover bones to make a rich broth. I prefer thighs and breast pieces that still have their skin and bones intact to achieve a more intense flavor. After searing the chicken, I typically keep the rendered fat in the pan. However, you can remove some or all of it and replace it with olive oil.

It's common practice to sear and cook the meat in the same pan that's been used for the onions and turmeric. This step helps the meat become infused with turmeric, which is believed by Iranians to reduce the gaminess of the meat.

Stews are prepared covered, over low heat, for an extended duration. Paying attention to details like the fit of the lid and the heat intensity can make a big difference. Also, it's important to know how to make adjustments to achieve the desired texture and consistency of the stew, especially when nearing the end of cooking. What you're looking for is best visualized by imagining a plate with fluffy rice on one side and stew on the other. A little of the broth should drift toward the rice and coat its bottom layer, but the rice should not appear to be drowning.

Add a little water or broth and turn the heat down if your stew is getting dry, especially if it's sticking on the bottom. Turn the heat up a touch and remove the lid if there seems to be too much liquid.

As with any dish, be attentive to the cooking process at every stage, taste frequently, follow your instincts, and make the necessary adjustments. That's how to build your skills and acquire what Iranians call *dast pokht*, meaning "the skillful hand in cooking."

HERBS

There is nothing subtle about the quantities of herbs used by Iranians. While other cuisines measure herbs in pinches and tablespoons, Iranian cuisine measures them in bunches and cups. In many ways, herbs are treated just like any other vegetable ingredient.

Preparing fresh herbs begins with separating the bunches into individual stems, followed by a thorough soak or rinse in the sink and then laying them out on a kitchen towel to dry. A salad spinner can expedite this process.

The next step is stemming the herbs based on their texture, type, and growth patterns. With herbs like mint, basil, tarragon, and savory, only the leaves are chosen, the stems being discarded entirely. Typically, parsley leaves are removed from their tough stems, which are discarded except for the tender top 2–3 inches (5–7.5 cm). Cilantro, on the other hand, boasts soft, flavorful stems, so only the bottom 1–2 inches (2.5–5 cm) of them need to be removed. Dill's mostly soft stems are retained, discarding only any particularly thick and dense parts.

In this book, quantities of herbs in the ingredient lists are specified in lightly packed cups of stemmed herbs.

The extent of subsequent chopping depends on the specific dish. Some recipes require finely processed herbs, leaving no visible or recognizable elements, such as in ghormeh sabzi. In contrast, herbs are coarsely chopped for most āshes and kukus, creating a textured appearance. Given the large quantities involved, I often use a food processor, but a cutting board and a good chef's knife work well, too. Chopped fresh herbs can be stored in the freezer, preserving their quality for up to a month.

Before the advent of greenhouses, Iranians would cultivate herbs during the warmer seasons, harvest them in fall, and dry them in vast quantities for use year-round. Over time, the cuisine not only adapted to but actively celebrated the intensity of these dried herbs. When dried, herbs like mint, fenugreek, dill, and even cilantro offer a distinctive pungency, and the dried form frequently became the preferred choice for many recipes.

Soaking dried herbs for at least 15 minutes is recommended, followed by draining them before use. If you're using dried herbs as a substitute for fresh, a general guideline is to use one-third the quantity and remember that the flavor profile is very likely to be different.

Khoresh Fesenjun

CHICKEN IN POMEGRANATE AND WALNUT SAUCE

MAKES 4 SERVINGS • GF

Some time ago, I conducted a cooking demonstration at one of Seattle's annual cultural festivals. As I walked through the steps to prepare khoresh fesenjun, I described my mother spending hours in the kitchen making this dish. Lacking a food processor, she prepared the walnuts by hand—choosing each walnut one by one, placing it on a wooden tray, and carefully smashing it with a hefty river rock before moving on to the next nut.

As I spoke, I noticed tears welling up in the eyes of one of the attendees. After the demonstration, we had a conversation, and she conveyed how my words had stirred memories of her own mother and the countless hours she had dedicated to cooking and caring for the family.

That day, I gained a deeper understanding of the power of food and storytelling, a reminder that love and dedication are as crucial in cooking as ingredients and techniques. I'll forever link khoresh fesenjun with that demo, and with the image of my mother crushing one walnut at a time.

- 2 cups (200 g) walnuts
- 2 tablespoons neutral oil, plus more as needed
- 4 chicken thighs (about 1½ lb/680 g total), bone in and skin on
- 1 onion, diced
- ½ cup (120 ml) pomegranate molasses, plus more to taste
- ½ cup (120 ml) water
- ½ teaspoon sea salt
- ¼ teaspoon ground black pepper
- 2-4 tablespoons (25-50 g) sugar (optional)
- ½ teaspoon saffron threads, ground and bloomed in 1 tablespoon hot water

Begin by taking out your food processor. Put the walnuts in the food processor bowl and process them until finely ground. Set aside.

Place a large enameled Dutch oven on the stove over medium-high heat. Add the oil and wait for it to shimmer before carefully adding the chicken pieces, skin side down. Sear the chicken until it becomes golden and crispy and renders some fat, about 5 minutes on each side. Remove the chicken from the pot, place it on a plate, and set aside.

You can leave the chicken fat in the pot or remove it. However, if you decide to discard the fat, you will need to add 2 more tablespoons of oil to sauté the onion in the next step.

With the heat set to medium, add the onion and sauté until it becomes aromatic and lightly golden, about 10 minutes.

CONTINUED

NOTES

Pomegranate molasses flavors vary by brand, so start with a small amount that can be adjusted during cooking. Alternatively, create your own pomegranate syrup by simmering 4 cups (960 ml) of unsweetened pomegranate juice with 2 tablespoons of fresh lemon juice over low heat for around 2½ hours to replace both the molasses and water.

I love making fesenjun because it reminds me to be patient and committed. While the stew simmers, it needs occasional stirring. The walnuts slowly thicken the stew as they soak up the liquid. To prevent crusting, use a flat wooden spatula to stir and, if available, a flame tamer to even out the heat and reduce the risk of burning.

For variations, try using almonds instead of walnuts and, for a vegan option, replace the chicken with roasted delicata squash and oyster mushrooms.

Using a rubber spatula, transfer the ground walnuts from your food processor bowl to the pot with the onion. Sautéing the walnuts lightly at this stage is crucial for enhancing their flavor. While walnuts are naturally rich and fatty, they tend to absorb the oil in the pot. So, reduce the heat to medium-low and stir continuously for 2–3 minutes. The walnuts should be well mixed with the onion and appear slightly dense and sticky.

Add the pomegranate molasses, water, salt, and pepper and stir to make sure everything is well combined. Return the seared chicken pieces to the pot and press them down to fully immerse them in the sauce. Partially cover the pot with the lid and raise the heat just enough to encourage the stew to simmer gently. When you notice the stew bubbling, reduce the heat to low and cover it with the lid.

After about 40 minutes, taste the sauce to assess the developing flavors. You're aiming for a robust pomegranate flavor with a balanced sweet and tart profile. If needed, add more pomegranate molasses, a couple of tablespoons at a time, to enhance the pomegranate flavor. You can also add a bit of sugar if you prefer a sweeter stew.

Let the stew simmer until the sauce becomes intensely rich and takes on a deep maroon color, while the chicken turns tender and easily falls off the bone. This step will take up to another hour. Finish the dish by adding the bloomed saffron.

Turn the heat off, keep the pot covered, and let it stand for 10 minutes. You'll notice how the natural oil from the walnuts and chicken will separate from the sauce and rise to the top. That's a sign of a khoresh that is *jā-oftādeh*, a Persian culinary term for a well-prepared and set stew.

Gently remove the chicken pieces, one by one, and place them in a serving dish. Drizzle the sauce over the chicken. Serve with a pot of steamed basmati rice.

Khoresh Ghormeh Sabzi

BEEF AND HERB STEW

MAKES 4 SERVINGS • GF

Khoresh ghormeh sabzi is a prime example of Iranians' obsession with herbs, but it also contains a massive contradiction. It uses about 6 cups (180 g) of chopped fresh herbs jam-packed with healthy green goodness. But the herbs are then sautéed in oil for nearly half an hour until they neither look brilliantly green nor carry a nutritional punch. Instead, they're transformed into a profoundly aromatic, dark green, and naturally sweetened version of their former selves. The nutrients are sacrificed for the sake of flavor.

FOR THE KIDNEY BEANS

⅔ cup (140 g) dried red kidney beans, soaked overnight and drained

4 cups (960 ml) water

FOR THE STEW

2 tablespoons olive oil

1 large onion, diced

1 teaspoon ground turmeric

1 lb (450 g) beef chuck or round, cut into 1-inch (2.5-cm) pieces

3 cups (720 ml) water

1½ teaspoons sea salt, divided

½ teaspoon ground black pepper

4 limu omāni (Persian dried limes), cut in half

2 tablespoons fresh lemon juice, or to taste

Let's start with the kidney beans, since they take some time to cook. Select a pot and add the beans and water. Bring to a boil over high heat and remove any foam that may have surfaced. Reduce the heat to low, cover, and cook until the beans are fully cooked and soft, about 1 hour. Once cooked, strain the beans in a colander and set them aside.

To make the stew, while the beans cook, place a Dutch oven over medium heat, add the oil, and sauté the onion until it becomes lightly golden, about 10 minutes. Stir in the turmeric, sautéing it for 2 minutes.

Increase the heat to medium-high, add the beef to the pan, and sauté until it's lightly browned, about 5 minutes. Pour in the water, add ½ teaspoon of the salt, cover, and bring it to a gentle simmer. Reduce the heat to low and let it simmer for 45 minutes.

To prepare the sabzi, as the beef and beans simmer in the background, place the parsley, cilantro, green onions, and spinach in your food processor and pulse until you have a very finely chopped mixture. Remove the herb mixture with a rubber spatula and set aside briefly while you set up for the next and most crucial step of the recipe: sautéing the herbs.

CONTINUED

FOR THE SABZI (HERBS)

4 cups (120 g) fresh parsley

2 cups (60 g) fresh cilantro

8 green onions or 1 small leek, trimmed and roughly chopped

½ cup (30 g) spinach

6 tablespoons (90 ml) olive oil, plus more as needed

2 tablespoons dried fenugreek leaves

NOTES

Take your time preparing for this stew, which includes washing, drying, stemming, and chopping all the herbs. I also recommend sautéing the herbs patiently to allow their flavors to fully develop. While increasing the heat may seem like a shortcut, it could result in the herbs developing a bitter and unappealing taste.

If you can't find limu omāni, you can enhance the tartness by adding extra freshly squeezed lemon juice to suit your taste.

To save time, you can use canned kidney beans instead of dried ones. Rinse them and add them when incorporating the limu omāni into the stew.

This dish can be made with lamb or chicken instead of beef. To make it vegan, use carrots, squashes, mushrooms, or even roasted eggplants instead of the meat.

Select a large frying pan and heat it over medium-high heat, then add the oil. Toss in the herb mixture, grab a wooden spatula, and be prepared for what is about to be nothing short of a magical transformation. Keep the heat on medium-high initially as you stir the herbs. After 5 minutes, drop the heat to medium-low as you continue to stir for another 15–20 minutes. This is the most intricate part of the dish; the herbs need to begin drying out while slowly developing a darker color and more intense aroma. Keep stirring as you keep a watchful eye on the herbs. If they are browning too fast, you may need to reduce the temperature, and if you find they are beginning to stick to the bottom, just add a bit more oil. Patience is a great virtue when sautéing herbs!

Remove from the heat, toss in the fenugreek leaves, stir, and set aside.

Once the beef has been cooking for 45 minutes, add the beans, herb mixture, remaining 1 teaspoon of salt, pepper, limu omāni, and lemon juice. Give everything a good stir, cover, and simmer over low heat for 45 minutes.

Adjust the stew by adding a small amount of water if needed. Keep in mind that this stew should be moist but not watery. Taste and adjust the stew for seasoning by adding more salt or lemon juice as needed. Turn the heat off and let the stew stand for 10 minutes before serving.

Congratulations on making khoresh ghormeh sabzi, one of the most iconic and beloved Iranian stews! This is a true accomplishment. Transfer the stew to a large serving bowl and accompany it with a steaming pot of basmati rice to soak up all of the delicious flavors. Or serve with a side of creamy plain yogurt for an extra touch of tangy flavor.

Khoresh Rivās

BEEF AND HERB STEW WITH RHUBARB

MAKES 4 SERVINGS • GF

Spring in the Pacific Northwest brings warmer weather and the prospect of fresh, new vegetables. Of these, I most eagerly anticipate rhubarb, which grows remarkably well in our temperate climate.

Khoresh rivās is another Iranian stew that celebrates the abundance of fresh herbs and sour flavors. Unlike the rest of the world, where rhubarb is almost always sweetened with sugar or strawberries, Iranians use rhubarb in savory dishes precisely because of its sour flavor.

6 tablespoons (90 ml) olive oil, divided

1 large onion, diced

1 teaspoon ground turmeric

1 lb (450 g) beef chuck or round, cut into 1-inch (2.5-cm) pieces

2½ cups (600 ml) water

1½ teaspoons sea salt, divided

6 cups (180 g) finely chopped fresh parsley

2 cups (60 g) finely chopped fresh mint

1 tablespoon dried mint

½ teaspoon ground black pepper

3 stems rhubarb, 12 inches (30 cm) each, cut into 1-inch (2.5-cm) pieces

Heat a Dutch oven over medium-high heat, add 2 tablespoons of the oil, and sauté the onion until it turns lightly golden, about 10 minutes. Sprinkle in the turmeric and sauté for a couple of minutes before adding the beef pieces to the pot. Raise the heat to medium-high and sauté the mixture until the beef is lightly browned, about 5 minutes.

Pour in the water, add ½ teaspoon of the salt, and bring the mixture to a simmer. Once you start seeing bubbles break the surface, reduce the heat to low, cover, and simmer for 1 hour.

While the stew simmers in the background, we can sauté the herbs. Heat a large frying pan over medium-high heat, then add the remaining 4 tablespoons (60 ml) of oil. As the oil spreads in the pan and begins to shimmer, add the parsley and fresh mint and begin stirring.

When the moisture from the herbs has largely evaporated, about 5 minutes, reduce the heat to medium-low while maintaining a constant stir. You'll notice the herbs becoming more fragrant, shrinking in size, and deepening in color to a richer green over the next 10 minutes. In the final minute, stir in the dried mint. Turn off the heat and set the pan aside for the time being.

After the beef has cooked for 1 hour, add the remaining 1 teaspoon of salt, the pepper, and the sautéed herbs. Stir, cover, and cook for another 30 minutes over low heat. The stew should be fragrant and the meat fork-tender at this stage.

Finally, add the rhubarb pieces to the stew, gently mix, cover, and cook until the rhubarb has softened, about 15 minutes. Take extra care not to overmix because rhubarb can fall apart quickly. Taste the stew and make any last-minute seasoning adjustments as needed.

Turn off the heat and let the stew stand for 10 minutes before serving. Transfer the stew to a serving bowl and accompany it with steamed basmati rice.

NOTES

For a vegan option, swap the beef with white beans, roasted tofu, or tempeh.

Baghāli Ghātogh

FAVA BEANS WITH POACHED EGGS AND CRISPY SHALLOTS

MAKES 4 SERVINGS4 • V GF

This dish is inherently simple but packed with a wide range of flavors. The distinctive notes of garlic and dill steal the spotlight, blending perfectly with the creamy beans and tender poached eggs. If I were to pick one dish to treasure forever, without a doubt, it would be this one.

¼ cup (60 ml) olive oil

8 cloves garlic, minced

1 teaspoon ground turmeric

1 package (14 oz/400 g) double-peeled frozen fava beans, thawed, or 2 cans (15 oz/425 g each) butter beans, drained and rinsed

1¼ teaspoons sea salt, divided

½ teaspoon ground black pepper

¼ cup (10 g) dried dill

2 cups (480 ml) water, plus more as needed

½ cup (120 ml) neutral oil

2 large shallots, thinly sliced into rings

4 eggs

Preheat a frying pan over low heat, add the olive oil, and gently sauté the garlic until it takes on a light golden hue, about 2 minutes. Sprinkle in the turmeric, sautéing it for another minute.

Add the beans, 1 teaspoon of the salt, pepper, dill, and water and give it a stir. Gently stir the beans so that they don't break apart. Cover and simmer over low heat for about 15 minutes.

While the beans are cooking, prepare the shallots. Place the neutral oil in a small saucepan and heat over medium heat until it begins to shimmer, 3–5 minutes. Carefully add the shallots, stirring occasionally, and cook until they turn golden, 7–8 minutes. Using a slotted spoon, remove the shallots from the oil and place them on a paper towel–lined plate. Sprinkle with the remaining ¼ teaspoon of salt and set aside.

Taste the beans and adjust the seasoning as needed while also checking for consistency. The beans should be moist, with enough liquid, but not overly watery.

Use a spoon to pull back some of the beans, creating four small wells, and carefully crack an egg into each. Sprinkle a pinch of salt and pepper over the eggs. Cover and cook over medium-low heat for 5 minutes, or longer if you prefer your eggs more well cooked.

CONTINUED

Carefully transfer the baghāli ghātogh to a serving dish, nestling the eggs on top. Generously sprinkle the fried shallots over the dish. Enjoy with steamed basmati rice or flatbread and a side of tangy yogurt. I hope you love this dish as much as I do!

> **NOTES**
>
> *The dried dill may be substituted with ⅔ cup (20 g) of chopped fresh dill if you prefer. Adjust the amount to suit your personal preference.*
>
> *Remember to reserve the leftover sautéed shallot oil; it's great for a tasty salad dressing when mixed with balsamic or red wine vinegar.*

Nargesi

SPINACH AND HERBS WITH POACHED EGGS

MAKES 4 SERVINGS · V GF

Nargesi, a humble but scrumptious dish, is something I'd enjoy for breakfast, lunch, or dinner any day! It's another classic from the Caspian Sea region, known for its bountiful produce, vegetables, and abundant use of eggs.

¼ cup (60 ml) olive oil

1 onion, diced

4 cloves garlic, minced

1 teaspoon ground turmeric

9 cups (540 g) coarsely chopped fresh spinach

1 cup (30 g) coarsely chopped fresh parsley

½ cup (15 g) coarsely chopped fresh mint

1 teaspoon sea salt

½ teaspoon ground black pepper

4 eggs

Heat a large frying pan over medium heat, add the oil, and sauté the onion until it turns a light golden color, about 10 minutes.

Stir in the garlic and turmeric and sauté for 2 minutes to layer in more flavor and color.

Add the spinach and toss it around in the pan, making sure it gets coated with the onion, garlic, and turmeric. Keep cooking until the spinach wilts and you notice liquid being released, about 5 minutes.

Toss in the parsley and mint and season with the salt and pepper. Once everything is well combined, cover the pan, reduce the heat to medium-low, and cook for 15 minutes.

Now, let's make some space for the eggs. Use a spoon to pull back some of the spinach, creating four small wells. Crack an egg into each of these wells. Sprinkle a pinch of salt and pepper on top of each egg.

Cover the pan again and let it cook over low heat until the eggs are cooked but still soft and slightly runny, about 5 minutes. You can increase the cooking time by another minute or two if you prefer your eggs well done.

Transfer it to a serving platter, softly placing the eggs on top, and serve with flatbread or steamed basmati rice.

> **NOTES**
>
> *Spinach can sometimes have a gritty or chalky texture. To remedy that, I like to add fresh herbs like parsley and mint to enhance the texture and add more flavor and aroma.*

Khoresh Bij Bij

BEEF STEW WITH POACHED EGGS

MAKES 4 SERVINGS • GF

Bij bij, a stew from the Caspian Sea region, was the first dish I ever made as a teenager. It's one of my all-time favorite comfort foods. Flavorful but simple, it can be made in about an hour with minimal effort.

During my vegetarian years, I found creative ways to prepare bij bij, whether by using crumbled tempeh or homemade seitan—both excellent meat alternatives—or store-bought meat substitutes.

¼ cup (60 ml) olive oil

1 onion, diced

4 cloves garlic, minced

1 teaspoon ground turmeric

1 lb (450 g) ground beef

¼ cup (60 g) tomato paste

2 Yukon gold potatoes, cut into 1-inch (2.5-cm) cubes

4 tomatoes (about 2 lb/900 g total), finely diced

1½ cups (360 ml) water

1½ teaspoons sea salt

½ teaspoon ground black pepper

2 tablespoons āb ghureh (unripe grape juice) or fresh lemon juice

4 eggs

Heat a large frying pan over medium-high heat, pour in the oil, and sauté the onion until it turns lightly golden, about 10 minutes.

Stir in the garlic and turmeric and sauté for an additional 2 minutes.

Place the ground beef in the pan, breaking it up into smaller pieces as you go. Sauté over medium-high heat until the meat lightly browns, 8–10 minutes.

Stir in the tomato paste and sauté for another 2 minutes to deepen the tomato flavor.

Add the potatoes, tomatoes, water, salt, pepper, and āb ghureh to the pan and stir. Once it starts to simmer, reduce the heat to low, cover, and cook until the potatoes become tender, about 40 minutes.

CONTINUED

At this point, we need to make some space for the eggs. Using a spoon, push the meat mixture aside to create four little wells for the eggs. Crack the eggs, one at a time, into the spaces you've created. Sprinkle a little more salt and pepper over the eggs and put the lid back on. It's really up to you how runny or firm you want your eggs. So, just play it by ear and cook them to your liking. I cook mine for 5 minutes.

Transfer the stew to a serving platter, taking extra care to keep the eggs intact. Serve with flatbread or steamed basmati rice, a side of yogurt, and fresh herbs.

> **NOTES**
>
> *Get playful by adding veggies like carrots, cauliflower, mushrooms, or sweet potatoes. Elevate the flavor profile with paprika, cumin, coriander, cinnamon, or chili powder.*

Jody's Mediterranean Chicken

CHICKEN STEW WITH ROASTED PEPPERS AND PRUNES

MAKES 4 SERVINGS • **GF**

Jody was my very first client as a personal chef, and I had the privilege of preparing meals for her every Monday morning for over a decade. Among her preferred dishes, a standout was this chicken stew, which she requested again and again.

When she retired, Jody decided to delve into the realm of cooking for herself. She first enrolled in my comprehensive, intuitive plant-based cooking class, covering the fundamentals of meal preparation. As my class repertoire expanded to Iranian cuisine, she joined me again, displaying a keen interest in the Iranian dishes I had prepared for her so many times.

We stayed in contact as the years passed, though we only saw each other infrequently. But we did have one more deep interaction, sadly in a somber context—a farewell conversation when Jody was reaching the end of a courageous battle against terminal cancer. In this moment, we both expressed the profound impact the other had made on us. This personal and memorable encounter underscored the significance of our connection through food. This is for Jody.

2 tablespoons olive oil

4 chicken thighs (about 1½ lb/680 g total), bone in and skin on

1 large onion, thinly sliced

2 cloves garlic, minced

1½ teaspoons sea salt

½ teaspoon ground black pepper

1 tablespoon smoked paprika

1 cup (240 ml) water

Heat a large frying pan over medium heat, pour in the oil, and carefully add the chicken pieces, skin side down. Cook until they are lightly browned, about 5 minutes on each side. Remove the chicken from the pan and set aside.

To the same pan, add the onion and sauté over medium heat for about 10 minutes. Add the garlic and continue to sauté for a couple more minutes.

Transfer the sautéed chicken pieces and any accumulated juices back to the pan and sprinkle with the salt, pepper, and paprika before adding the water. Cover the pan and let everything cook over low heat for 45 minutes.

Preheat the oven to 450°F (230°C).

CONTINUED

- 2 red bell peppers
- 1 cup (130 g) prunes, pitted
- 1 cup (120 g) green olives, sliced
- 1 tablespoon fresh lemon juice
- 1 tablespoon chopped fresh cilantro

While the chicken is cooking, we'll work on the red peppers. Place them on a baking sheet, transfer to your preheated oven, and roast until they're nicely blistered and blackened, about 25 minutes. Once the peppers are done, remove them from the oven and put them in a paper bag or a bowl covered with plastic wrap as they cool down. This will help with the peeling process.

Once the peppers are cool, remove the skin and seeds, then slice the peppers into long strips. Make sure to save any juices that come out during this process, as they're full of flavor.

Now, get the peppers and their juices into the pan, along with the prunes, olives, and lemon juice. Stir, cover, and cook for another 15 minutes. Be sure to taste and adjust the seasonings to your liking.

Transfer to a serving bowl and garnish with a sprinkle of cilantro. Serve with a bowl of quinoa and a simple leafy green salad for a satisfying meal.

Khoresh Hulu

PEACH AND SAFFRON CHICKEN STEW

MAKES 4 SERVINGS • GF

At the heart of this dish are the peaches, their flavors magnificently enhanced by a generous infusion of high-quality saffron.

The aroma of ripe peaches takes me straight back to my culinary school days and my first encounter with Colorado peaches at the farmers' market in Boulder. Their quality was unparalleled, transforming the kitchen of my culinary school into a peach perfume shop—a truly unforgettable experience.

Among Colorado peaches, those from Palisade stand out as some of the best. Renowned for their unmatched ripeness, sweetness, and "chin-dripping juice," these gems appear at roadside stands throughout the state.

2 tablespoons olive oil

4 chicken thighs or breasts (about 1½ lb/ 680 g total), bone in and skin on

1 onion, diced

1 teaspoon ground turmeric

1 cup (240 ml) water

1 teaspoon sea salt

2 tablespoons unsalted butter or ghee

3 peaches, stoned but not peeled and cut into ½-inch (12-mm) slices

½ teaspoon ground black pepper

¼ teaspoon ground cinnamon

Juice of 1 lime

2 tablespoons unrefined cane sugar, or to taste

1½ teaspoons saffron threads, ground and bloomed with 2 tablespoons hot water

2 sprigs fresh mint

Preheat a Dutch oven over medium-high heat, add the olive oil, and carefully place the chicken pieces, skin side down, in the pan. Allow them to sear until they turn lightly golden and crispy, about 5 minutes per side. Once done, remove the chicken from the pot and set aside.

To the same pot, add the onion and sauté until it turns light brown, about 10 minutes. Sprinkle the turmeric in and sauté for about 2 minutes.

Pour the water into the pot and return the seared chicken and any accumulated juices to the pot. Sprinkle in the salt and bring to a gentle simmer. Reduce the heat to low, cover, and simmer for 1 hour. During this time, you can prepare the peaches.

Place the butter in a frying pan and sauté the peaches over medium-low heat until they develop a gentle caramelization, about 2 minutes on each side. Be careful not to overcook them, as they will continue to cook later in the stew. Remove from the heat and set aside.

CONTINUED

After the chicken has simmered for 1 hour, it's time to add the pepper, cinnamon, lime juice, and sugar.

Cover and continue to cook over low heat until the chicken is fork-tender, about 20 minutes. This is a good time to taste the stew and adjust the seasoning to your liking, paying attention to the balance of sour and sweet.

Gently place the sautéed peach slices on top of the chicken, drizzle the saffron water over them, and give the pot a gentle shake. Simmer for another 10 minutes.

To serve, delicately transfer the chicken from the pot to a serving bowl, generously drizzle with the sauce, and arrange the peaches on top. Garnish with the mint and accompany with steamed basmati rice and a light leafy green salad.

NOTES

For this stew, I choose slightly underripe peaches to keep their texture intact.

You can swap chicken for beef or lamb, or to make it vegetarian, use chickpeas, pan-seared tofu, or seitan chunks—they all work wonderfully.

Khoresh Kalleh Gonjeshki

PETITE MEATBALLS WITH CRISPY POTATOES

MAKES 4 SERVINGS4 • GF

The Persian name for these meatballs perfectly represents their small and delicate nature: *kalleh gonjeshki* translates to "little bird's head."

FOR THE MEATBALLS

1 lb (450 g) ground beef

1 small onion, grated

1 teaspoon sea salt

½ teaspoon ground black pepper

1 tablespoon dried mint

½ teaspoon ground turmeric

¼ teaspoon ground cinnamon

2 tablespoons olive oil

FOR THE SAUCE

2 tablespoons olive oil

1 onion, diced

4 cloves garlic, minced

1 teaspoon ground turmeric

2 tablespoons tomato paste

2 tomatoes, diced

¼ cup (60 ml) fresh lemon juice

1 cup (240 ml) water, plus more as needed

1 teaspoon sea salt

½ teaspoon ground black pepper

To make the meatballs, combine all of the ingredients except the olive oil in a large mixing bowl. Mix thoroughly and shape the mixture into small meatballs, about 1 tablespoon each.

Heat a large frying pan over medium-high heat. Add the oil and sauté the meatballs, turning and moving them as needed, until they are evenly browned, 8–10 minutes. Once done, remove the meatballs from the pan and set them aside. Depending on the size of your frying pan, you may need to do this step in batches.

To start the sauce, add the olive oil to the same pan and sauté the diced onion over medium heat until it becomes lightly golden, about 10 minutes. Add the garlic and turmeric, sautéing for an additional 2 minutes.

Stir in the tomato paste and sauté for another 2 minutes to layer in more flavor.

Finally, add the tomatoes, lemon juice, water, salt, and pepper and bring the mixture to a gentle simmer.

Return the sautéed meatballs to the pan, cover it, and cook over low heat for 1 hour. Taste and adjust the consistency, tartness, and seasoning to your preference.

While the stew is simmering, preheat the oven to 350°F (180°C).

CONTINUED

FOR THE POTATOES

3 large Yukon gold potatoes, cut french fry style

¼ cup (60 ml) olive oil

½ teaspoon sea salt

½ teaspoon ground black pepper

½ teaspoon ground turmeric

To prepare the potatoes, place them in a mixing bowl, add the oil, salt, pepper, and turmeric and toss to coat. Transfer the mixture to a baking sheet and roast until the potatoes turn golden on the outside and become tender on the inside, 30-35 minutes. Be sure to flip them halfway through.

When ready to serve, arrange the stew on a serving platter and place the roasted potatoes on top. Serve with steamed basmati rice and a side of fresh herbs and creamy yogurt.

NOTES

Ground lamb or ground turkey may be substituted for beef. Keep in mind that ground turkey can be dry and dense. To improve the texture of turkey meatballs, try adding 2 tablespoons of quick oats to the mixture.

Give yourself plenty of time to patiently roll small and even meatballs!

NOTES

I opted for fresh herbs for this recipe due to their easy availability, but traditionally, dried herbs are used. With dried herbs, use just one-third of the amount you'd use for fresh herbs.

Zucchini or yellow squash, cut into larger pieces, are great alternatives to using eggplant in this dish.

You can salt the eggplants for 30 minutes before cooking for a more tender and luscious texture.

Melā Ghormeh

EGGPLANT WITH HERBS AND POACHED EGGS

MAKES 4 SERVINGS • V GF

Locally sourced or foraged ingredients, such as herbs, unripe grapes, bitter oranges, and pomegranates, enrich northern Iranian dishes. Melā ghormeh highlights such local ingredients, creating a unique, complex flavor.

½ cup (120 ml) olive oil, divided

1 onion, diced

1 teaspoon ground turmeric

6 cloves garlic, minced

2 Italian eggplants, peeled and cut into ½-inch (12-mm) cubes

2 tomatoes, diced

2 tablespoons tomato paste

2 cups (60 g) finely chopped fresh parsley

½ cup (15 g) finely chopped fresh mint

½ cup (120 ml) āb ghureh (unripe grape juice) or fresh lemon juice

1 teaspoon sea salt

½ teaspoon ground black pepper

1 cup (240 ml) water

4 eggs

Heat a large frying pan over medium heat, add 2 tablespoons of the oil, and sauté the onion until it turns a light golden color, about 10 minutes. Add the turmeric and garlic and sauté for 2 minutes. Remove everything from the pan and set aside.

Heat the remaining 6 tablespoons (90 ml) of oil in the same pan over medium heat. Place the eggplants in the pan and cook until they are lightly browned and somewhat softened, about 10 minutes. Remember to stir, but be careful not to overmix.

Return the sautéed onion mixture to the pan along with the tomatoes, tomato paste, parsley, mint, āb ghureh, salt, pepper, and water. Gently stir, reduce the heat to low, cover, and simmer for 15–20 minutes.

While the eggplant mixture is simmering, make sure there is enough liquid left in the pan to poach the eggs. If it seems dry, add a little bit of water. Taste and adjust for seasoning.

To make room for the eggs, use a spoon to move aside the eggplant mixture and make four wells. One at a time, crack the eggs into the spaces you've created. Sprinkle a little more salt and pepper on top of the eggs and put the lid back on. You can make your eggs as soft or firm as you like. I usually go for 5 minutes.

Transfer the stew to a platter, keeping the eggs intact, and serve with flatbread or steamed basmati rice, a side of yogurt, and fresh herbs.

Khoresh Gheymeh

BEEF AND YELLOW SPLIT PEA STEW WITH CRISPY POTATOES

MAKES 4 SERVINGS • GF

To me, this dish represents an Iranian take on the classic meat and potato comfort dish, with a few unique ingredients, of course! Persian dried limes, or limu omāni, provide a bold, tangy citrus taste with deep, earthy, fermented undertones.

FOR THE YELLOW SPLIT PEAS

½ cup (100 g) yellow split peas, rinsed

1½ cups (360 ml) water

FOR THE STEW

2 tablespoons olive oil

1 large onion, diced

1 teaspoon ground turmeric

1 lb (450 g) beef chuck or round, cut into ½-inch (12-mm) pieces

¼ cup (60 g) tomato paste

1½ cups (360 ml) water, plus more as needed

1½ teaspoons sea salt, divided

3 limu omāni (Persian dried limes), halved

½ teaspoon ground black pepper

1 teaspoon sugar

¼ teaspoon saffron threads, ground and bloomed in 2 tablespoons hot water

To prepare the split peas, select a small pot, add the split peas and water, and bring it to a gentle boil. Keep an eye on the pot, as yellow split peas produce lots of foam and can spill over. Once boiling, partially cover and simmer over low heat for about 20 minutes. The split peas will be partially cooked at this stage and will continue to cook some more when added to the stew. Remove from the heat, strain, and set aside.

To make the stew, heat a large Dutch oven over medium heat, add the oil, and sauté the onion until it turns a light golden color, about 10 minutes. Sprinkle in the turmeric and stir until the onion turns golden and aromatic, about 2 minutes.

Raise the heat to medium-high, add the beef, and cook, stirring, until lightly browned, about 5 minutes.

Stir in the tomato paste and sauté over medium heat for a couple of minutes. Be sure not to skip this step because sautéing brings out the flavor of the tomato paste. Pour in the water and add ½ teaspoon of the salt. Bring it to a gentle simmer, then reduce the heat to low, cover, and cook for 30 minutes.

CONTINUED

FOR THE POTATOES

3 large Yukon gold potatoes, cut french fry style

¼ cup (60 ml) olive oil

½ teaspoon sea salt

½ teaspoon ground black pepper

½ teaspoon ground turmeric

NOTES

Although the traditional method involves frying the potatoes, I personally favor roasting them in the oven, especially with convection, if it's an option, or using an air fryer.

For a vegan option, use more yellow split peas and add eggplants, mushrooms, or carrots for extra flavor and texture, omitting the beef.

If dried limes aren't available, use fresh lemon juice to achieve the desired tartness.

Toss in the limu omāni, remaining 1 teaspoon of salt, pepper, and sugar. Give it a stir and simmer for another 30 minutes.

Preheat the oven to 350°F (180°C).

To prepare the potatoes, place them in a mixing bowl, add the oil, salt, pepper, and turmeric, and toss to coat. Spread the potatoes on a baking sheet in a single layer and roast them until they turn golden and crispy, 30–35 minutes. Be sure to flip them halfway to get them crispy on both sides.

After the potatoes are in the oven and the stew has simmered for an hour, add the partially cooked yellow split peas to the stew. Give it a stir, cover, and simmer for another 15 minutes.

At this stage we want the beef to be tender and the yellow split peas holding their shape. The stew should be dense and packed with ingredients, and the broth should be visible but not too runny. If you find there is still too much liquid, push the lid a little to the side and raise the heat to evaporate some of the excess. Alternatively, if you find the stew on the drier side, just add a touch more water. Be sure to taste the stew and adjust the seasoning to your preference.

Add the saffron water, stir, remove the stew from the heat, and allow it to stand for 10 minutes.

Scoop the stew into a large serving dish, garnish with the crispy potatoes, and accompany it with a steaming pot of basmati rice. A dollop of creamy plain yogurt on the side adds a touch of tangy richness that perfectly complements the hearty flavors of the stew.

Khoresh Morgh Torsh

CHICKEN IN TANGY WALNUT AND HERB SAUCE

MAKES 4 SERVINGS • GF

Morgh torsh is a hearty chicken stew from the Caspian Sea region, highlighting many of the classic characteristics of Iranian stews. Finely ground walnuts bring richness and texture. Citrus provides a balancing tartness, while herbs contribute fresh, intricate flavors.

- 4 cups (120 g) fresh parsley
- 4 cups (120 g) fresh cilantro
- 1 cup (30 g) fresh mint
- 6 green onions, trimmed and roughly chopped
- 1 cup (100 g) walnuts
- 6 tablespoons (90 ml) olive oil, divided
- 4 chicken thighs or breasts (about 2 lb/900 g total), bone in and skin on
- 1 onion, finely diced
- 1 teaspoon ground turmeric
- 2 cups (480 ml) water, plus more as needed
- 1½ teaspoons sea salt
- ½ teaspoon ground black pepper
- ½ cup (120 ml) fresh lemon juice, plus more to taste

Place the parsley, cilantro, mint, and green onions in a food processor. Pulse until you have a finely chopped mixture. Transfer the herbs to a mixing bowl using a rubber spatula.

Process the walnuts into a finely ground consistency using the same food processor and set aside in a small bowl.

Heat a large Dutch oven over medium heat. Add 2 tablespoons of the olive oil to the pot and carefully place the chicken pieces inside, skin side down. Sear the chicken until it's lightly browned, about 5 minutes per side. Remove from the pot and set aside on a plate.

Add the onion to the same pot and sauté over medium heat until lightly golden, about 10 minutes. Add the turmeric and sauté for an additional 2 minutes. Remove the onion from the pan and add it to the plate with the seared chicken.

Returning to the same pot, add the remaining 4 tablespoons (60 ml) of olive oil and the herb mixture. Sauté over medium-high heat, stirring constantly, for a couple of minutes. Reduce the heat to low as the herbs dry out and become highly aromatic, cooking for another 15–20 minutes. Once the herbs start to lightly brown, add the ground walnuts and stir for another minute. Add a touch more oil if necessary to make sure the mixture doesn't stick to the pot and burn.

CONTINUED

Pour in the water and add the salt and pepper, along with the reserved chicken and onion. Stir, cover, and bring it to a gentle simmer. Reduce the heat to low and cook for 1 hour. Next, add the lemon juice and continue to cook until a rich, dense sauce has developed, 20–30 minutes. Taste and adjust the consistency and seasonings as needed.

Remove from the heat and keep the pot covered for 10 minutes before serving. Serve with steamed basmati rice or flatbread and a side of yogurt.

> **NOTES**
>
> *To make a vegan version, omit the chicken and add 1 cup of cooked yellow split peas near the end. Alternatively, you can serve the stew on a bed of hearty roasted root vegetables.*

Khoresh Gojeh Bādemjān

EGGPLANT AND TOMATO STEW WITH SOUR GRAPES

MAKES 4 SERVINGS • **VG GF**

In the culinary world, there's a remarkable harmony between certain vegetables. Nothing exemplifies this better than eggplants and tomatoes, a duo celebrated in this recipe and across diverse global cuisines. The addition of unripe grapes creates pleasant tartness and acidity that amplifies the familiar flavors of tomatoes and eggplants.

2 Japanese eggplants

1 tablespoon plus ½ teaspoon sea salt, divided

¾ cup plus 2 tablespoons (210 ml) olive oil, divided

1 onion, diced

1 teaspoon ground turmeric

2 cloves garlic, minced

2 tablespoons tomato paste

½ teaspoon ground black pepper

⅔ cup (160 ml) water

¼ cup (45 g) ghureh (unripe grapes)

4 tomatoes (about 2 lb/900 g total), quartered

Peel the eggplants and cut them lengthwise into ½-inch (12-mm)-thick slices. Depending on the length of the eggplant, you may want to cut the slices in half to ensure they fit well in the frying pan. Sprinkle the eggplant slices with 1 tablespoon of the salt and let them stand for 30 minutes. Using a paper towel, wipe off the salt and the excess moisture.

Heat a large frying pan over medium-high heat and add ¼ cup (60 ml) of the oil. The oil should heat up quickly and start shimmering. Carefully arrange half the eggplant slices in a single layer in the pan. Reduce the heat to medium-low and let the eggplants cook undisturbed on one side until they turn nicely brown, about 10 minutes. Flip the eggplants, add another 2 tablespoons of the oil, and continue cooking for another 5 minutes. Remove the first batch of eggplants from the pan and set them aside.

CONTINUED

Repeat the process with the remaining eggplants, using 6 tablespoons (90 ml) of the oil in total.

Add the remaining 2 tablespoons of oil to the same pan and sauté the onion over medium heat until it becomes lightly browned, about 10 minutes.

Add the turmeric and garlic to the pan and continue to sauté for 2 minutes. Stir in the tomato paste, add the remaining ½ teaspoon of salt and the pepper, and sauté for another 2 minutes.

Pour in the water, add the ghureh and tomatoes, and stir to mix. Cover the pan, reduce the heat to low, and simmer for 15 minutes.

Place the sautéed eggplants into the stew, gently pressing them down into the sauce, and cook for another 30 minutes over low heat.

Taste and adjust the seasoning and the liquid level as needed. The stew should have some liquid but not be overly watery.

Serve alongside steamed basmati rice with a side of yogurt for a light and satisfying meal.

> **NOTES**
>
> *Ghureh (unripe grapes) are available in fresh, frozen, or brined forms at Iranian or Mediterranean markets. Alternatively, 2–4 tablespoons (30–60 ml) of fresh lemon juice can be a suitable replacement.*

CHAPTER 7

KABABS, BURGERS, AND FISH

Tempeh Burger with Mango Salsa • **VG**
168

Grilled Saffron Chicken Kababs • **GF**
Jujeh Kabāb • 171

Grilled Lamb Kababs • **GF**
Kabāb Kubideh • 174

Salmon with Za'atar and Herb Sauce • **GF**
177

Broiled Halibut with Tamarind and Herb Sauce • **GF**
178

Stuffed Fish with Herbs and Barberries • **GF**
Māhi Shekam Por • 179

VG • VEGAN   **GF** • GLUTEN FREE

THE THERAPIST WITHIN

SEATTLE, WA | 2001

Therapy wasn't emphasized in my upbringing, so for many years the idea of it was completely foreign to me. However, in 2001, when several aspects of my life—my career, relationship, and questions of identity—were undergoing significant changes, I reached a tipping point, and that's when therapy became my refuge.

Walking into my therapist's office for the first time was intimidating. I entered with a laundry list of grievances and untold stories, uncertain of what lay ahead. Yet, my therapist, Doniella, became my lifeline, a caring and supportive figure who not only helped me through the difficult times in my life but also inspired me to pursue a career as a therapist myself.

I can still recall Doniella's therapy room, nestled in her house, filled with natural light and offering a breathtaking view of her garden's vibrant colors and lush scenery. Holding a warm cup of tea in my hands, I gradually started to unpack the hidden chapters of my life.

Doniella's tender presence and gentle but impactful words resonated deeply. One by one, I unraveled the unresolved and challenging issues that burdened me. When the time finally arrived, I mustered up the courage to open up about the experiences I had endured during the Iranian Revolution and its aftermath. Doniella was the first person I ever told about the boy soldier aiming his rifle at my chest. Something changed as I wept on her couch, and for the first time I witnessed Doniella shedding tears as well.

My experience with Doniella was genuinely transformative. It was a journey of healing, love, and understanding that planted a seed within me, propelling me toward the path of becoming a therapist myself. Witnessing the care and support she provided, I started thinking about how a total stranger could significantly influence another person's life and well-being. In therapeutic terms, we call this attachment repair, where a therapist shows up to help clients heal their emotional injuries. Doniella became that figure in my life, and I aspired to be that person for others. I decided to pursue a graduate program in psychotherapy.

Training to become a therapist perfectly complemented my roles in the culinary world. As a personal chef, I had witnessed the transformative power of nutritious, whole foods on my clients' overall health. As a culinary teacher, I had expanded my repertoire to deliver classes that emphasized the emotional and relational aspects of food and eating, including one designed specifically for cancer survivors. My training in psychotherapy gave me a set of skills for listening and understanding, and made me a better teacher and storyteller.

Continuing to cook and teach while I built my therapy practice, I also refined my own relationship with food, adopting a more flexible approach to address some health issues. At this time, I incorporated ethically raised animal protein back into my diet.

I also had the wonderful opportunity to return to my graduate school, this time as a faculty member teaching courses on the psychology of nourishment, foundations of counseling for dieticians, and culinary skills for nutritionists.

> **Until you make the unconscious conscious, it will direct your life and you will call it fate.**
>
> —DR. CARL JUNG

Nearly twenty years later, my path crossed once again with Doniella's when she subleased an office next to mine. Now both much older, we shed our former therapist-client roles and formed a deep friendship rooted in kindness, respect, and the joy of reconnection. I remained in touch with Doniella until she passed away.

TEMPEH BURGER WITH MANGO SALSA

MAKES 4 SERVINGS • VG

Tempeh is a natural, unadulterated product that can be easily transformed into tasty and nourishing plant-based dishes. I have always enjoyed tempeh, but my appreciation for it grew even more after I learned how to make it from scratch. I particularly enjoy experimenting with ways to prepare, shape, and transform this otherwise unassuming soy product.

FOR THE BURGERS

- 1 package (½ lb/225 g) tempeh
- 1 small shallot, quartered
- 2 cloves garlic
- 1 inch (2.5 cm) piece of fresh ginger, peeled and roughly chopped
- ¼ cup (8 g) fresh cilantro
- ½ cup (50 g) rolled oats
- 2 tablespoons tapioca flour, plus more as needed
- 2 tablespoons tamari
- 1 tablespoon rice vinegar
- 1 tablespoon toasted sesame oil
- 2 tablespoons brown sugar
- ¼ teaspoon chipotle pepper powder
- 3 tablespoons neutral oil, divided

To make the burgers, cut the tempeh into quarters, place it in a steamer basket over boiling water in a pan, and steam it for 10 minutes. This will partially cook the tempeh and make it easier to digest. Remove the tempeh and set it aside to cool.

While the tempeh is cooling, place the remaining ingredients except the neutral oil in a food processor and process until a coarse paste forms.

Crumble the tempeh by hand and add it to the food processor. Pulse the mixture just long enough until the tempeh pieces are no longer visible and become homogeneous. Test the consistency of the mixture by taking a small piece and checking whether it holds together. If it's too crumbly, add another 1 tablespoon of tapioca flour.

Remove the mixture from the food processor and shape it into four patties, each about ¼ inch (6 mm) thick. Place the patties in the fridge for 30 minutes to chill and help them maintain their shape.

CONTINUED

FOR THE SALSA

1 large mango, peeled, pitted, and diced

1 small red bell pepper, seeded and finely diced

¼ red onion, finely diced

¼ cup (8 g) coarsely chopped fresh cilantro

1 small jalapeño pepper, seeded and minced

2 cloves garlic, minced

Zest and juice of 1 lime

¼ teaspoon sea salt

To make the salsa, while the patties are chilling, combine all the ingredients in a mixing bowl. Give it a good toss and refrigerate until you are ready to serve.

To cook the burgers, heat a large cast-iron pan over medium heat. Add 2 tablespoons of the oil and swirl to coat the pan. Place the patties in the pan and reduce the heat to medium-low. Cook until nicely browned on one side, about 5 minutes. Flip the patties over, add the remaining 1 tablespoon of oil, and cook for another 5 minutes.

Serve on their own with the salsa, or get some buns and top the burgers with a generous portion of the salsa and any additional toppings or condiments of your choice.

> **NOTES**
>
> *In place of mango, good options for the salsa include pineapple, papaya, kiwi, and watermelon.*

Jujeh Kabāb

GRILLED SAFFRON CHICKEN KABABS

MAKES 4 SERVINGS · GF

Jujeh kabāb delivers remarkably colorful, tasty, and tender chicken pieces. Marinating the chicken in a mixture of saffron-infused yogurt for an extended period not only makes the meat tender but also gives it the distinctive color and vibrant flavor of saffron.

1 teaspoon saffron threads, ground and bloomed with 6 tablespoons (90 ml) hot water, divided

2½ lb (1.1 kg) boneless and skinless chicken breasts or thighs, cut into 1-inch (2.5-cm) pieces

1 cup (240 ml) whole milk yogurt

1 onion, diced

2 tablespoons olive oil

1½ teaspoons sea salt

½ teaspoon ground black pepper

Juice of 2 limes, divided

1 tablespoon unsalted butter, melted

Start by pouring 4 tablespoons (60 ml) of the saffron water over the chicken in a large mixing bowl. Toss the chicken, cover, and refrigerate for 1 hour. During this time, the chicken will absorb the bright yellow-orange color, aroma, and flavor of saffron.

In a separate mixing bowl, combine the yogurt, onion, olive oil, salt, pepper, and juice of 1 lime. Add this mixture to the large bowl with the chicken and saffron mixture. Mix everything with a spatula, cover, and refrigerate it for at least 2 hours.

When you're ready to start cooking, preheat your grill.

Now it's time to skewer the chicken. Remove the marinated chicken from the fridge and thread the chicken pieces onto metal or soaked wooden skewers, pushing them through one by one. The number of pieces on each skewer will depend on the skewer's length. Try to avoid overcrowding the chicken pieces on the skewer. Place the skewers on a large platter or baking sheet, and tap the skewers gently against the tray to remove any excess marinade. Discard the remaining marinade.

CONTINUED

Prepare the baste by whisking together the melted butter, the remaining 2 tablespoons of saffron water, and the juice of 1 lime in a small bowl.

Place the skewers on the grill over direct heat and grill on both sides, turning and basting the kababs regularly, until the internal temperature of the chicken pieces has reached 165°F (74°C), 8–10 minutes. The grilling time may vary based on your grill's temperature and strength.

Remove the kababs from the grill and place on a clean platter.

Serve jujeh kabāb with grilled vegetables, your choice of flatbread, or alongside a pot of steamed basmati rice.

> **NOTES**
>
> *Give the chicken ample time to marinate in the yogurt mixture, aiming for at least 2 hours if overnight isn't possible.*
>
> *When using wooden skewers, soak them in water for 15 minutes before threading the chicken to keep them from burning.*
>
> *Plan ahead and prepare your charcoal or gas grill well in advance to ensure it's hot and ready. To prevent the chicken from sticking to the grill grates, use a paper towel and a pair of tongs to lightly oil the grates with a neutral oil before grilling.*

Kabāb Kubideh

GRILLED LAMB KABABS

MAKES 4 SERVINGS • GF

Mention *kabab* to an Iranian, and you inevitably evoke deep and sentimental memories. Kabāb kubideh, in particular, is highly regarded for its distinctive texture and flavor profile, making it one of the most popular kabab options.

1 onion, grated, with the juice squeezed out and reserved

1 lb (450 g) ground lamb

1 teaspoon sea salt

½ teaspoon ground black pepper

1 tablespoon unsalted butter

1 tablespoon onion juice, from above

1 tablespoon fresh lemon juice

In a mixing bowl, combine the onion with the lamb, salt, and pepper. Thoroughly knead the mixture for about 5 minutes until you get a smooth paste. This crucial step binds the meat proteins and fat and ensures the meat sticks to the skewers.

Once the mixture is ready, place it in the fridge for 30 minutes to allow it to marinate and rest.

If you're using a charcoal grill, start the coals 30 minutes before grilling the kabObs. For a gas grill, turn it on 15 minutes in advance to reach a temperature of about 450°F (230°C).

Divide the meat mixture into four equal parts, molding each portion into an oval-shaped piece 4–5 inches (10–13 cm) long.

Now, we'll form the kababs on the skewers. Dampening your hands frequently with the spare onion juice will help prevent the meat from sticking to your hands.

Take a skewer in one hand and one portion of the meat mixture in the other. Place the meat mixture next to one edge of the skewer, then slowly squeeze the meat mixture onto both sides of the skewer. Continue to stretch and squeeze the meat mixture along the skewer until you have a kabab that is 6–7 inches (15–18 cm) long and ½–⅔ inch (12–17 mm) thick, with the skewer in the middle. Squeeze firmly to ensure the meat mixture is firmly attached.

CONTINUED

NOTES

Lamb can be substituted with beef. Look for a leanness of 80–85 percent if possible; this ensures an ideal texture for the meat to stick to the skewer.

A crucial aspect of preparing these kababs is the kneading technique. The meat and other ingredients should be kneaded for about 5 minutes, creating a sticky mixture that adheres to the skewer and retains its shape during grilling.

You'll need 1-inch (2.5-cm) wide flat skewers for making kabāb kubideh.

The traditional way to cook the kababs is by suspending them over hot coals without a grill grate, to prevent sticking. You can modify a gas grill by placing bricks or metal pipes on opposite sides to create a ledge for the skewers to rest on, at least 1½ inches (4 cm) tall, to avoid contact with the grill grate.

Using your thumb and index finger, gently press into the meat mixture to create uniform indentations about 1 inch (2.5 cm) apart. This is a traditional design, and also helps ensure that the meat is pressed well onto the skewers.

Suspend the kabab over a baking sheet, letting the skewer ends rest on the edges of the sheet. Repeat this process to prepare the remaining kababs.

Prepare your baste by melting the butter in a small saucepan and mixing in the onion juice and lemon juice.

Now, it's time to grill the kababs, remembering to baste them on both sides throughout the process.

Suspend the skewers (see Notes) directly over the heat and flip them over within 15 seconds. This will help ensure even cooking on both sides and prevent the meat from slipping off. After a few rotations, grill each side for about 4 minutes. They should be seared and browned on the outside while still juicy inside.

Finally, place the kababs on a serving platter. To remove them from the skewers, gently press them off using a large piece of flatbread or a serving fork.

Kababs are best enjoyed alongside flatbread, steamed basmati rice, butter, sumac, fresh herbs, and raw onions. In keeping with tradition, you can enhance the rice's creaminess and richness by adding a single egg yolk and butter directly to the steaming hot rice, combining them immediately.

SALMON WITH ZA'ATAR AND HERB SAUCE

MAKES 4 SERVINGS • **GF**

When I first moved to Seattle, I was astounded by the abundance of the Pacific Northwest. Not only did it offer outstanding natural beauty, but it also delivered produce that—as someone who loves to cook—I was excited to explore. One of the things that stood out most was fresh salmon.

I prepared salmon for my first Thanksgiving in Seattle to honor my new home. It was a special moment embracing the traditions and rituals of my new community. I'm grateful to live in such a beautiful place, which has been my home now for over thirty years. This dish is dedicated to the Emerald City.

FOR THE SALMON

6 cups (1.4 l) water

¼ cup (50 g) sea salt

4 (6-oz/170-g each) salmon filets

2 tablespoons olive oil

½ teaspoon ground black pepper

FOR THE ZA'ATAR HERB SAUCE

½ cup (120 ml) olive oil

¼ cup (60 ml) fresh lemon juice

Zest of 1 lemon

4 cloves garlic

1 teaspoon sea salt

¼ teaspoon ground black pepper

1 cup (30 g) fresh parsley

½ cup (15 g) fresh dill

½ cup (15 g) fresh chives

2 tablespoons za'atar

Preheat the oven to 425°F (220°C).

To prepare the fish, use a large rectangular pan similar to one you might use for lasagna. Mix the water and salt in the dish, add the fish, and let it brine at room temperature for 15 minutes. After brining, remove the fish and pat dry with paper towels to remove any excess moisture. Brush each filet on both sides with the oil, sprinkle it with the pepper, and then place it on a baking sheet. Bake until the flesh of the fish flakes apart when you press down on it, 8–12 minutes, depending on the size of your filets.

To make the sauce, while the fish is baking, place all of the ingredients in a food processor and process until the sauce is reasonably smooth, up to 60 seconds. You will end up with about 1 cup (240 ml) of sauce.

When the fish is cooked to your liking, take it out of the oven and transfer it to a serving platter. Drizzle the sauce over the fish before serving. Serve the salmon with roasted vegetables or with a hearty salad for a satisfying light meal.

> **NOTES**
>
> *The za'atar herb sauce can be made ahead to save some time. If you have any left over, keep it in the fridge for up to 5 days and use it as a dressing for roasted vegetables or salads. Here's another chance for improvisation—experiment with various herb combinations, paired with lime juice, orange juice, or robust vinegars.*

BROILED HALIBUT WITH TAMARIND AND HERB SAUCE

MAKES 4 SERVINGS • **GF**

I'm a child of northern Iran, and the recipes in this book reflect that. However, it seems fitting to include a dish influenced by the flavors of southern Iran. This region is celebrated for its creative use of tamarind, dates, distinctive regional spices, and the bounty of seafood from the Persian Gulf.

This particular sauce captures the essence of southern Iran, offering a spicy, mildly sweet tang that perfectly complements the rich, creamy texture of halibut. My friend Zahra Razeghi, from the Persian Gulf region, generously shared her insights and provided guidance on how to prepare this sauce.

FOR THE SAUCE

¼ cup (60 ml) olive oil, plus more as needed

1 large shallot, minced

4 cloves garlic, minced

¼ teaspoon ground turmeric

¼ teaspoon red chile pepper powder

2 cups (60 g) finely chopped fresh cilantro

1 tablespoon dried fenugreek leaves

1 tablespoon tomato paste

1 tablespoon tamarind concentrate

2 Medjool dates, finely chopped

½ teaspoon sea salt

1 cup (240 ml) water

FOR THE FISH

4 (6-oz/170-g) halibut filets

2 tablespoons neutral oil

1 teaspoon sea salt

To make the sauce, grab a frying pan and heat it over medium-low heat, then add the oil. Sauté the shallot until lightly browned, about 5 minutes, then incorporate the garlic, turmeric, and chile pepper. Sauté the mixture for another 2 minutes. Toss in the cilantro, increase the heat to medium, and keep stirring until it becomes aromatic and slightly darkened, roughly 10 minutes. If the herbs become dry or stick to the pan, add a touch more oil. Add the fenugreek and tomato paste, stirring for another minute to enhance their flavors.

Finally, it's time to add the tamarind, dates, salt, and water. Bring the sauce to a gentle simmer, reduce the heat to low, cover, and cook until the sauce has become dark, highly aromatic, and quite punchy with flavor, about 30 minutes. Be sure to taste the sauce and adjust the seasoning to your preference.

To prepare the fish, start preheating the broiler when the sauce is nearly done. Brush both sides of the halibut filets with the oil, sprinkle the salt evenly on both sides, and place them on a baking sheet. Broil until the halibut flakes easily with a fork, 5–7 minutes, depending on the size. Place the halibut filets on a serving platter and drizzle the sauce on top.

NOTES

Tamarind paste can be pretty potent, so start with 1 tablespoon, taste, and add more if needed. You can substitute the halibut with cod, red snapper, or prawns.

Māhi Shekam Por

STUFFED FISH WITH HERBS AND BARBERRIES

MAKES 2 SERVINGS • GF

Having decided to introduce this stuffed fish dish to one of my cooking classes, I began testing the recipe in my Seattle kitchen. As I cooked, I realized that it had been a staggering thirty-eight years since my last taste of it. Still, it felt like I was preparing it purely from my memory of the flavors.

As I ate, every mouthful—filled with the lively pop of fish roe, the barberries' zesty tang, and the fresh herbs' unmistakable fragrance—evoked more memories. A vivid image came to me: my ten-year-old self, marveling at my mother's culinary talents during one of her unforgettable dinner parties. In those days, a grand feast would feature a colossal fish generously stuffed and sewn shut to preserve its precious filling.

I searched through my photo albums recently, longing to discover a snapshot of our dining table in Tehran adorned with that magnificent centerpiece. Alas, the sole evidence of those cherished events resides in my memory.

FOR THE FISH

1 whole branzino, butterflied and deboned (about 1½ lb/680 g), or any other seasonally available, white-fleshed fish

2 teaspoons sea salt, divided

1 cup (30 g) fresh parsley

1 cup (30 g) fresh cilantro

½ cup (15 g) fresh mint

½ cup (15 g) fresh basil

1 cup (100 g) walnuts

1 small onion, grated, juice squeezed out and discarded

2 tablespoons fresh lime juice

4 cloves garlic, minced

Preheat the oven to 400°F (200°C) while you gather your ingredients and equipment.

To prepare the fish, rinse it under cool water, then pat it dry with paper towels.

Season the fish evenly inside the cavity and over the outer skin with 1 teaspoon of the salt. Set aside.

To prepare the stuffing, place the herbs in a food processor and process them until they are finely chopped. Using a rubber spatula, transfer the herbs to a large mixing bowl.

Process the walnuts in the same food processor until they are finely ground. Remove them from the food processor and add them to the herb mixture.

Combine the remaining ingredients, including the remaining 1 teaspoon of salt, with the herb mixture and mix well.

CONTINUED

½ teaspoon ground black pepper

½ cup (75 g) dried apricots, chopped

½ cup (30 g) dried barberries, rinsed

2 oz (50 g) tobiko or other fish roe

FOR THE GLAZE

½ teaspoon saffron threads, ground and bloomed with 2 tablespoons hot water

2 tablespoons olive oil

To stuff the fish, take the herb mixture and carefully press it into the fish cavity until all of the stuffing has been used. Make sure to distribute it evenly and fill the fish cavity.

Secure the stuffing inside the fish by wrapping the fish with some kitchen twine. Cut four segments of twine, each about 8 inches (20 cm) long. Grease a baking sheet lightly and space the twine segments a few inches apart on the sheet. Place the stuffed fish on top of the twine segments and bring the edges of the butterflied fish together. Tie the twine around the fish to make sure the stuffing stays securely inside.

To make the glaze, in a small mixing bowl, combine the saffron water and olive oil. Brush the glaze evenly over the top skin side of the fish to create a beautiful golden color and add flavor to the fish.

Place the fish in the oven to bake. When done, the flesh should be firm and flaky and the internal temperature should reach 140°F (60°C), 20–30 minutes. Let the fish stand for 5 minutes before removing the twine.

Māhi shekam por can be served with sabzi polo (see page 119), Iranian herb rice, or plain steamed basmati rice. Garnish with fresh herbs and slices of fresh oranges and limes.

CHAPTER 8

BREADS

Savory Cheese Pastries • V
Fatayer Jebneh • **187**

Iranian Flatbread • VG
Nān Barbari • **189**

Arab Bread • VG
Khobez Arabi • **192**

Iranian Sourdough Flatbread Baked on Hot Pebbles • VG
Nān Sangak • **194**

V • VEGETARIAN   **VG** • VEGAN

RECONNECTION

SAN JOSE, CA, AND SEATTLE, WA | 2014–2017

In an instant, the stage was engulfed in darkness, only to be illuminated again by a dazzling array of lights. The volume soared to ear-splitting decibels as the familiar chords reverberated through the air, leaving me breathless.

It had been over thirty years since I had found myself surrounded by so many Iranians. As I glanced around, I saw a sea of people with the same dark hair and complexion, and it warmed my heart to realize that I was not an outsider.

After a lengthy instrumental introduction, the person who had brought us all together for this profoundly nostalgic experience finally stepped onto the stage. It was none other than Googoosh!

To Iranians, Googoosh represents so much from the days before the 1979 Revolution: freedom, glamor, fashion, joy, and cherished memories. To this day, she remains the most celebrated Iranian pop singer. Googoosh was intertwined with my childhood and represents the Iran I once knew and loved.

The emotions welled up, and I found myself teary-eyed and sniffling while singing and dancing as if I were the same ten-year-old who had watched her on TV so many times. Surprisingly, I could still recall most of the lyrics to her songs.

The concert was incredibly moving and marked the beginning of a considerable shift within me. But it took more than this single event to prompt me to reconnect with Iran.

At around the same time as my reintroduction to Googoosh, I found myself deeply affected by a wave of growing anti-immigrant sentiment, including the implementation of a ban on travel and refugee resettlement from selected countries with predominantly Muslim populations. Iran, once more, took center stage in the news, with the then-existing nuclear deal hanging in the balance and looming threats of additional sanctions. All of this weighed heavily on my mind, worrying my days and disturbing my nights.

Giving up on sleep in the early hours of one morning, I gravitated toward the kitchen. I wasn't prompted by hunger, nor by a desire for emotional eating (a struggle I've faced at times in my life). Rather, I felt an innate need for comfort and solace through the power of working with food and cooking.

I rummaged through the pantry for ingredients and inspiration, eventually deciding to make tortillas. For me, there's a primal power in getting my hands into the food, manipulating it and watching it spring to life. As I felt the texture of the flour, kneaded the dough, rolled out each tortilla, baked them one by one, and absorbed their aroma, I found myself deeply appreciating the whole process.

This experience caused me to recognize once again that the act of preparing food holds immense significance for me. It involves making thoughtful decisions about ingredients, selecting the cooking method, and fully immersing myself in the sensory experience—taste, touch, scent, sight, and sound. Engaging in this culinary mindfulness becomes deeply fulfilling and helps anchor me in the present moment.

> *We cannot selectively numb emotion. If we numb the dark, we numb the light. If we take the edge off pain and discomfort, we are, by default, taking the edge off joy, love, belonging, and the other emotions that give meaning to our lives.*
>
> —DR. BRENÉ BROWN

Also around this time, many of my therapy clients were struggling to cope with changes in the political landscape. One in particular felt stuck and overwhelmed by feelings of despair and hopelessness. Although he found meditation and support from his community to be helpful, he was still searching for something that would give him a sense of empowerment.

At one point in our conversation, I asked him to reflect on what skills and gifts he had to offer. Suddenly, he paused, stiffened his posture, sat taller, and proudly announced that he would do something he was good at: offering healing Reiki sessions to those who felt similarly stuck due to current events.

Witnessing this revelation, I realized that I, too, had a passion I could use both to empower myself and to bring about positive change. I would start teaching culinary skills again, but this time it wouldn't be about plant-based intuitive cooking; I would focus exclusively on Iranian cuisine. I would introduce and share positive aspects of Iranian culture to combat the negative messages being spread at that time. This was the beginning of a theme that continues through the writing of this book: food as a gentle form of activism.

Although I possessed a reasonable proficiency in Iranian cuisine, I recognized the need to delve deeper and thoroughly understand the intricate techniques involved in preparing Iranian dishes. I aspired to achieve the level of expertise known as *dast pokht* (meaning "the skillful hand in cooking" in Persian), masterfully blending ingredients and techniques, creating a harmonious symphony of flavors, textures, and presentation.

Also, if I was going to be showcasing Iranian culture, I knew that I would need to confront the obstacles that had kept me distant for many years. I had to embrace all of the feelings and emotions I had exiled for the past three decades, making myself vulnerable to gain a deeper sense of connection to my identity and cultural heritage.

Fatayer Jebneh

SAVORY CHEESE PASTRIES

MAKES 8 PASTRIES • V

Fatayer jebneh, Arabic cheese pastries, make a great snack or light meal. This recipe is a gift from my friend Nadia Tommalieh, a culinary instructor who generously shares her love and expertise in Palestinian and Arabic cuisine. This recipe stands out as one of my favorites among the numerous gems in her baking classes. I've made subtle adjustments to Nadia's original recipe.

FOR THE DOUGH

1½ cups (185 g) all-purpose flour, plus more for dusting

½ cup (60 g) whole wheat flour

½ teaspoon (3 g) sea salt

¼ cup (60 g) whole milk, at room temperature, plus more for brushing the dough

7 tablespoons (105 g) lukewarm water

1½ teaspoons (8 g) sugar

1½ teaspoons (5 g) active dry yeast

2 tablespoons (30 g) olive oil

NOTES

I know that many home cooks in the United States measure dry ingredients by volume (in measuring cups and spoons), but for bread baking, I recommend weighing them for accuracy.

To make the dough, combine the flours and salt in a mixing bowl and set it aside.

In a separate mixing bowl, whisk together the milk, water, sugar, yeast, and olive oil. Cover the bowl with a clean kitchen towel and let it stand at room temperature until the yeast has bloomed and formed foam on top, about 5 minutes.

Gradually add the flour and salt mixture to the yeast mixture and mix with a spatula until the dough starts to come together.

Transfer the dough to a lightly floured surface. Shape it into a ball and knead it until you have a smooth, soft texture, 8–10 minutes.

Divide the dough into eight equal pieces, roll each piece into a ball, and place on a baking sheet lightly dusted with flour. Cover with a clean kitchen towel and let the dough balls rise at room temperature (about 70°F/21°C) until they double in size, about 1 hour.

While the dough is rising, preheat the oven to 450°F (230°C), line a baking sheet with parchment paper, and prepare the cheese filling.

CONTINUED

BREADS | 187

FOR THE CHEESE FILLING

6 oz (170 g) halloumi cheese, soaked in cool water for 10 minutes

6 oz (170 g) fresh mozzarella cheese

1 egg, at room temperature, lightly beaten

1 teaspoon Aleppo pepper

1 teaspoon nigella seeds

¼ cup (8 g) finely chopped fresh parsley

1 teaspoon olive oil

FOR FINISHING

¼ cup (60 ml) olive oil

2 tablespoons coarsely chopped fresh parsley

To make the cheese filling, use a paper towel to pat dry the halloumi and mozzarella cheeses, then grate them into a mixing bowl. Add the egg, Aleppo pepper, nigella seeds, chopped parsley, and olive oil and mix using a rubber spatula.

To assemble the fatayer, sprinkle some flour on your countertop. Using a floured rolling pin, roll a dough ball into an oval shape, about 4 by 6 inches (10 by 15 cm) across and about ⅛ inch (3 mm) thick. Spread 2–3 tablespoons of the cheese filling evenly in the center of the oval, leaving about 1 inch (2.5 cm) of space around the edges.

To shape the fatayer, we are aiming for a shape that resembles a canoe or a boat. Gently fold the longer sides of the dough oval over the sides of the cheese filling, leaving the center part exposed. Then, press the dough together at both ends, pinching the dough to make sure it's completely sealed around the filling.

Repeat the process for the remaining fatayer, and place them on the prepared baking sheet, leaving about 1½ inches (4 cm) of space between them. Brush the dough with milk for some added color.

Place in the oven and bake until the bottom and top of the fatayer turn a light golden brown, 10–12 minutes. As a final step, put them under the broiler for some extra caramelization and color, about 1 minute, but be sure to keep an eye on them to avoid burning.

To finish, brush the pastries with olive oil, cover them with a clean kitchen towel, and let them rest for 5 minutes.

Sprinkle with parsley and serve the fatayer either warm or at room temperature, paired with your favorite salad.

Nān Barbari

IRANIAN FLATBREAD

MAKES 2 FLATBREADS • VG

During childhood visits to the Caspian Sea, we would always spend time with my uncle and aunt, Dāyi Reza and Zan Dāyi Badri. Each morning, we were welcomed by the irresistible aroma of fresh bread from the nearby bakery. Nān barbari was the perfect companion to locally produced butter, creamy feta cheese, and an array of homemade jams, creating the most spectacular breakfast spread.

FOR THE BREAD

2 cups (250 g) all-purpose flour, plus more as needed

½ cup (60 g) whole wheat flour

2¼ teaspoons (7 g) active dry yeast

1 teaspoon (5 g) sugar

¾ cup (180 g) water, at room temperature, divided

1 tablespoon (15 g) olive oil, plus more as needed

1½ teaspoons (8 g) sea salt

FOR THE TOPPING

1 tablespoon (8 g) all-purpose flour

¼ teaspoon baking soda

⅓ cup (80 g) water

1 teaspoon sesame seeds

1 teaspoon nigella seeds

To make the bread, grab a bowl and combine the flours, mixing them until they are incorporated. Set aside for the moment.

In another bowl, dissolve the yeast and sugar in ½ cup (120 g) of the water. Let it stand for a few minutes to allow the yeast to become active and foamy. Once the yeast is activated, add the remaining ¼ cup (60 g) of water, the oil, and the salt and stir.

Gradually add the flour to the wet mixture. Begin by adding 1 cup (125 g) of the flour, using your whisk to blend everything. Add the rest of the flour progressively, transitioning from the whisk to a spatula or, better yet, your hands.

Remember that it's easier to have a slightly wet dough to which you can add flour rather than a dry dough that requires more water. Once most of the flour is added, assess the dough's texture. If it's still somewhat sticky, incorporate the remaining flour until the dough becomes kneadable and doesn't stick to your hands.

Lightly sprinkle a work surface with flour and knead the dough until it becomes slightly stretchy and soft to the touch, with a gentle bounce back when pressed with a finger, 10–15 minutes.

Add 1 teaspoon of the olive oil to a clean, large bowl. Place your dough in the bowl, rotating the dough so that its entire surface gets lightly coated with oil.

CONTINUED

BREADS | 189

Cover the bowl with a towel and let the dough rise at room temperature (about 70°F/21°C) until it has doubled in size, about 1 hour. The dough should feel very soft to the touch at this stage.

Sprinkle a small amount of flour on your work surface. Gently remove the dough from the bowl and place it on the flour. Divide the dough into two equal pieces and shape each piece into a ball without overworking the dough. Cover with a towel and let the dough balls rest on the kitchen counter for 30 minutes.

While the dough rests, preheat the oven to 450°F (230°C) and line a baking sheet with parchment paper.

To make the topping, combine the flour, baking soda, and water in a small saucepan over low heat. Stir until the mixture thickens, 3–4 minutes, then remove from the heat.

Gently press and stretch each ball of dough to create an oval shape about 12 by 6 inches (30 by 15 cm). Carefully transfer one of the ovals to the prepared baking sheet.

Use your fingertips to create four parallel rows of indentations along the length of the oval. Brush the top of the dough with half of the flour and water mixture and sprinkle half of the sesame and nigella seeds on top.

Bake until the bread has turned a crispy, golden brown, 12–15 minutes. Once baked, remove from the oven and repeat the process with the remaining dough.

After cooling, store the nān barbari in an airtight container. It's best enjoyed while still warm, but you can also freeze it in an airtight bag for up to 3 months.

Khobez Arabi

ARAB BREAD

MAKES 10 FLATBREADS • VG

This recipe is also from my talented and passionate friend Nadia Tommalieh, an expert in Palestinian and Arabic food. As a student in her class, I gained insights into the profound significance of bread in Palestinian culture, reminding me how it holds an equally revered place in Iranian cuisine. I've made only subtle adjustments to her original recipe.

- 1½ teaspoons (5 g) active dry yeast
- 1 teaspoon (5 g) sugar
- 1½ cups (360 g) water, at about 100°F (38°C), divided
- 3¼ cups (370 g) all-purpose flour, plus more for dusting
- 1 cup (115 g) whole wheat flour
- 1½ teaspoons (8 g) sea salt
- 1 tablespoon (15 g) olive oil

Combine the yeast and sugar with ½ cup (120 g) of the water in a small mixing bowl. Cover and set it aside until it blooms and you see the yeast forming foam on top, about 5 minutes.

Sift the flours into a large mixing bowl. Using a rubber spatula, stir in the salt, olive oil, and yeast mixture. Gradually add the remaining 1 cup (240 g) of water to the mixture until the dough comes together, making sure all of the flour is fully incorporated. Keep in mind that you might not need to use all of the liquid. It's better to have a slightly moist dough rather than a dry one because the extra moisture helps the bread puff up during baking.

Transfer the dough from the bowl to a lightly floured surface. Shape it into a ball and knead it until you have a smooth, soft texture that isn't too sticky, 8–10 minutes.

Roll the dough into a log and divide it into ten equal pieces. Roll each piece into a ball and place the dough balls on a lightly floured flat surface or baking sheet. Cover with a clean kitchen towel and let the dough rise in a draft-free location until doubled in size, about 1 hour.

NOTES

Make sure to have plenty of clean kitchen towels handy, especially if you have limited counter space.

Instead of in the oven, you can make khobez arabi on the stovetop using a cast-iron skillet. Flipping the bread about every 20 seconds, cook until it puffs up, roughly 2 minutes in total.

Using a rolling pin dusted with flour on a lightly floured surface, roll out each ball into a disk 7–8 inches (18–20 cm) in diameter. Place the disks on a lightly floured surface. To save space, you can layer them, separating each layer with a clean kitchen towel. Cover them all with a clean kitchen towel and let the dough rest for 15 minutes.

While the dough rests, preheat the oven to 500°F (260°C) using a convection fan if available.

Place two disks on a baking sheet and put them in the oven. Bake for 4–5 minutes, keeping a close eye on them. They should rise and form a hollow pocket while becoming slightly browned on the outside. Transfer the baked bread to a plate or basket lined with kitchen towels and cover them. Let them rest for a few minutes before serving. Repeat with the remaining disks.

Arab bread is best enjoyed warm and should be covered to prevent it from drying out.

Alternatively, once cooled, you can store the bread in airtight bags in the fridge for 2–3 days or in the freezer for up to 3 months.

Nān Sangak

IRANIAN SOURDOUGH FLATBREAD BAKED ON HOT PEBBLES

MAKES 4 FLATBREADS • VG

In Persian, *sangak* means "little stone," and nān sangak is a traditional sourdough-based bread that's baked on a bed of hot pebbles. This recipe is from my friend Sahar Shomali, a skilled pastry chef and the proprietor of Kouzeh Bakery in Los Angeles.

Like many others, I turned to sourdough baking during the early days of the global pandemic in 2020. After some practice and confidence building, I was regularly baking all sorts of sourdough: nān sangak, sourdough pancakes, burger buns, and crusty whole wheat loaves. Often I would bake two loaves: one for my household, and one to help me stay connected with friends during those isolating days. I would jump on my bicycle or my motorbike and leave fresh, often still-warm loaves on friends' doorsteps throughout Seattle. I added nān sangak to my blog, and—once cooking classes had started up again—to my curriculum.

1 tablespoon (15 g) active sourdough starter (see Notes, page 196)

2 tablespoons (15 g) all-purpose flour

¾ cup plus 1 tablespoon (195 g) water, divided, at room temperature

1 cup plus 2 tablespoons (130 g) whole wheat flour

¾ cup plus 1 tablespoon (100 g) bread flour

1 teaspoon (5 g) sea salt

2 teaspoons sesame seeds

2 teaspoons nigella seeds

Mix the sourdough starter with the all-purpose flour and 1 tablespoon (15 g) of the water in a small jar, combining them fully. Loosely cover and set it aside in a warm spot, about 70°F (21°C), until it has doubled in size, 4–6 hours.

In a mixing bowl, combine the whole wheat and bread flours and remaining ¾ cup (180 g) of water and mix until a dough forms. Cover and let it rest for 10 minutes.

Add the sourdough starter mixture, wet your hand, and lift up one side of the dough, gently stretching it and folding it over itself. Rotate the bowl a quarter turn and repeat this process until the starter mixture is mostly incorporated, 6–8 turns. Cover and let it rest for 5 minutes.

Sprinkle the salt over the dough and repeat the stretching and folding process until the salt is incorporated, 6–8 turns. Cover and let it rest at room temperature (70°F/21°C) until it has doubled in size, about 3 hours.

Transfer the dough to the fridge and leave it to rest for 12–16 hours.

To bake the bread, fill a baking sheet with pebbles and place it on the lower rack of the oven. Preheat the oven to 525°F (275°C), or the highest setting available, and let the pebbles heat for at least 15 minutes.

As the oven heats, remove the dough from the fridge and divide it into four pieces.

You will need a small bowl of water and a large plate or platter to assemble and transfer the dough onto the pebbles. Wet your hands and add a tablespoon of water to the plate, creating a barrier to prevent the dough from sticking.

Place one piece of the dough on the wet plate and gently press and stretch it into an oval shape, about 10 by 6 inches (25 by 15 cm). Don't fuss over this; each flatbread will have its own unique shape! Let the dough rest for 5 minutes.

Very carefully remove the baking sheet from the oven. Being careful not to touch the hot pebbles, hold the plate over the baking sheet. Slowly tilt the plate so the dough begins sliding off the wet surface onto the pebbles. Pull the plate back in a smooth, slow motion, and help the remaining dough slide onto the pebbles. Don't attempt to rearrange the dough, as it will already be stuck to the stones.

Sprinkle a quarter of the seeds over the dough and place the baking sheet back in the oven. Bake until the bread is mottled brown, about 8 minutes.

CONTINUED

Remove the baking sheet from the oven and use tongs to transfer the bread to a cooling rack. There will always be some pebbles stuck to the underside of the bread. Once it has cooled, remove any remaining pebbles and ensure that none are embedded in the bread.

Repeat with the remaining pieces of dough and the seeds.

Nān sangak is best served fresh out of the oven. It can be stored in an airtight container in the freezer for up to 3 months. Reheat it before serving.

> **NOTES**
>
> *You will need natural pebbles that are not chemically treated, dyed, or coated. I purchased ordinary pea-size river pebbles from a home and garden store, washed them thoroughly, and tested them to ensure they could withstand high heat without cracking. To do this, I laid the pebbles on a baking sheet, placed another baking sheet on top, and baked them at 525°F (275°C) for 30 minutes.*
>
> *To make any type of sourdough bread, you'll need a sourdough starter, which you can purchase or obtain from a friend. But you can also cultivate one easily from water, flour, and a small piece of fruit. My friend Cynthia Lair, who has literally written the book on sourdough, recommends naming your starter to help you remain diligent in its care. Mine is called Golabi, the Persian word for pear, because that's the fruit I used. Golabi is now more than three years old, and has been shared with numerous sourdough enthusiasts.*

CHAPTER 9

DESSERTS

Saffron Carrot Halva • V GF
Halvā-ye Haviji • 203

Saffron and Lemon Olive Oil Cake • V GF
204

Rhubarb and Orange Blossom Scones • V
207

Saffron Ice Cream • V GF
Bastani Sonati • 209

Cardamom and Rose Water Cupcakes • V
Keyk Yazdi • 212

Silky Rose Rice Pudding • V GF
Ferni • 214

V • VEGETARIAN **GF** • GLUTEN FREE

CHAPTER 9

THE CASPIAN CHEF

SEATTLE, WA | 2017

Starting in 2017, I set out to craft the best Iranian cooking classes I could deliver.

To each of my classes, I would bring cherished Iranian cookbooks and a selection of distinctive Iranian spices and other ingredients. With great care and pride, I delicately laid out the items on a beautiful tapestry adorned with handcrafted Iranian pieces. Offering this glimpse into the richness of my Iranian heritage would inevitably pique curiosity and be a conversation starter.

I would also provide a list of local Iranian restaurants, shops, bakeries, and organizations and announcements of upcoming events.

As a welcoming gesture, I presented students with a plate of fresh herbs topped with sliced radishes, cucumbers, crumbled feta, and a handful of walnuts. This display of Iranian hospitality not only served as a refreshing appetizer, but it also set the perfect tone to kick off my three-hour classes.

These classes were the best possible stage for my storytelling. I'd begin by sharing my background and explaining why I'd chosen to shift my focus to Iranian cuisine. I'd add remarks about the dishes we were about to prepare. And I'd delve into a brief history of Iran, recounting anecdotes from the beloved Persian epic poem, *Shāhnāmeh*, which emphasizes the enduring power of light even after a millennium of darkness.

I was surprised and delighted by the evident thirst for knowledge about Iran's culture, traditions, and cuisine. Students eagerly asked in-depth questions, displaying a genuine interest in learning more about Iran. Conversations became more intense and would often continue long after the formal class session ended.

During this period, I also became a member, and later Culinary Board Director, of Seattle-Isfahan Sister City Advocacy (SISCA), a nonprofit group dedicated to fostering and normalizing human-to-human connections between these two remarkable cities. SISCA organized two major annual events. The first was a celebration at Seattle City Hall of Nowruz, the Iranian New Year. Drawing a crowd of nearly two thousand attendees, this event showcased the rich New Year rituals and broader Iranian culture.

SISCA's second key event was an annual gathering called Chefs Without Borders. This unique collaborative dinner was crafted by two chefs—one in Seattle and the other in Iran. Each chef meticulously prepared a multicourse meal designed by their counterpart in the other country. Guided by the iconic chef Tom Douglas, the event in Seattle blossomed into a vibrant occasion that drew about 150 guests. The corresponding event took place in either Isfahan or Tehran, where diners were introduced to dishes inspired by the wonderful cuisine of the Pacific Northwest.

Teaching several Iranian cooking classes each month and contributing to SISCA's activities made me feel good about my advocacy for Iranian culture. However, I sensed that there was more I could do to elevate my efforts. The question remained: What was my next step? I started to explore what it would take to write and—probably more challenging—actually publish a book. Predictably, it being 2019, I received advice to start a blog and to establish a social media presence.

Not only did these seem like daunting tasks in themselves, but they also required me to define a brand. While initially challenging, this process ultimately led me to a decision that still feels right today. I have a deep emotional connection to the Caspian Sea, on the shores of which I spent the happiest days of my childhood. I chose to call myself "the Caspian Chef."

Although there were already notable figures sharing Iranian recipes online, I aimed to emphasize two key aspects in my blogging efforts. First, I wanted my recipes to convey stories: narratives of family traditions, longings, and associated emotions. This mirrored my approach to teaching in-person classes, where I had found that human stories transcend borders. Second, I aimed to make Iranian cuisine more accessible to non-Iranians. While certainly discussing how dishes are prepared traditionally, I also highlighted substitutions and adjustments for readily available ingredients and personal preferences.

It was also important to me to continue the theme of gentle activism. I quickly discovered the potential of my social media platforms to foster connection and raise awareness. I collaborated with fellow chefs to host online fundraising and advocacy events, using the remarkable power of food to make a positive impact.

> *Build longer tables instead of higher walls.*
> —CHEF JOSÉ ANDRÉS

My affection for storytelling has always been strong. Stories possess a universal quality that imparts information about characters, emotions, and places. They serve as bridges for understanding, learning, and creating new connections. My blog and social media channels became vehicles for a tale: the story of a boy who left home long ago and continues to discover his identity through his love for food and deeply rooted desire for connection.

Halvā-ye Haviji

SAFFRON CARROT HALVA

MAKES 8–10 SERVINGS • **V GF**

Halva, a beloved confection, holds a special place in Iranian culinary heritage. Made with flour, syrup, and bright, uplifting spices, halva is deeply rooted in Iranian culture. While it's often associated with ceremonies and occasions, today, we celebrate its vibrant color and delicate flavor as a sweet treat, best enjoyed with a hot cup of tea.

4 carrots (500 g), cut into ¼-inch (6-mm) slices

1 cup (200 g) unrefined cane sugar

1½ cups (360 ml) water

¼ teaspoon sea salt

½ cup (120 ml) rose water

1 teaspoon saffron threads, ground and bloomed with 1 tablespoon hot water

1 cup (155 g) white rice flour

½ cup (115 g) unsalted butter

2 teaspoons ground cardamom

2 tablespoons pistachios, coarsely chopped

1 teaspoon crushed dried rose petals

Place the carrots in a saucepan and add the sugar, water, and salt. Bring the mixture to a boil over high heat, stirring just enough to dissolve the sugar. Once it starts boiling, reduce the heat to low, cover the saucepan, and let it simmer until the carrots have become tender, 15–20 minutes.

Transfer the carrots, along with any leftover syrup, to your blender. Add the rose water and saffron water and purée until you get a smooth and creamy texture. Set aside.

In a large frying pan, gently toast the rice flour over low heat for about 10 minutes, stirring constantly. Be very careful not to let it burn; you want the flour to turn aromatic and only lightly browned.

Add the butter and keep stirring until it has fully melted and been incorporated into the flour. Next, add the cardamom and the puréed carrot mixture. Take extra care as you add the puréed carrots, as they may splatter.

Continue stirring the mixture over low heat for another 10–15 minutes to integrate all of the flavors. At this point, the mixture should transform into a thick, smooth, paste-like consistency.

Transfer the halva to a plate, pie dish, or tart pan with a removable ring. Press it down firmly and use a rubber spatula to make the top surface even. Let the halva cool. Once it has, you can decorate the surface—using the back of a soup spoon or a paring knife—with simple patterns, such as lines, circles, or waves. Garnish with the pistachios and rose petals.

Halva can be enjoyed either chilled or at room temperature. Be sure to store it in the fridge, covered, to keep it fresh.

SAFFRON AND LEMON OLIVE OIL CAKE

MAKES 8 SERVINGS • V GF

This cake is a symphony of flavors, showcasing each ingredient's unique appeal. Its balance is a testament to what happens when carefully chosen ingredients unite in perfect harmony.

Olive oil is the star of this show, weaving its velvety smoothness and fruity essence into every crumb. The tangy freshness of lemon and the subtle taste of saffron are the perfect infusions of flavor. The delicate almond flour lends a nutty undertone and makes this an exceptionally light and moist cake.

FOR THE CAKE

2 cups (250 g) almond flour

½ cup (60 g) sorghum flour

1 teaspoon baking powder

¼ teaspoon baking soda

¼ teaspoon sea salt

4 large eggs, at room temperature

⅔ cup (140 g) unrefined cane sugar

½ cup (120 ml) extra-virgin olive oil

¼ cup (60 ml) fresh lemon juice

Zest of 1 lemon

1 teaspoon saffron threads, ground and bloomed with 1 tablespoon hot water

Position the rack in the lower third of the oven and preheat it to 350°F (180°C).

Line the bottom of an 8-inch (20-cm) cake pan with parchment paper and lightly grease the sides with melted butter or cooking spray to prevent sticking and ensure a smooth release after baking.

To make the cake, in a mixing bowl, combine the flours, baking powder, baking soda, and salt. Set aside.

Grab an electric hand mixer and a large mixing bowl. Crack the eggs into the bowl and mix them at low speed first before gradually increasing to high speed. Keep mixing until the eggs have developed a fluffy and airy texture, 45–60 seconds.

While continuously mixing on low speed, add the sugar, followed by the olive oil, lemon juice and zest, and finally, the saffron water. The egg mixture should be bright in color and still airy.

Slowly add the flour mixture to the eggs while mixing on medium speed. Mix until the batter is smooth and silky. Don't fret about overmixing, because there is no gluten in this cake.

Pour the batter into the prepared cake pan, place in the oven, and set a timer for 40 minutes.

CONTINUED

FOR THE ICING

½ cup (50 g) powdered sugar, sifted

1 tablespoon fresh lemon juice

Remember that this delicate, light cake needs you to leave the oven door closed until the time is up!

After 40 minutes, the cake should have risen slightly and become golden brown. Test for doneness by inserting a toothpick in the center; if it comes out clean, remove the cake from the oven. Let the cake cool to the touch on a wire rack, still in the pan.

To remove the cake from the pan, gently slide a butter knife along the sides, ensuring it separates the cake from the edges as you move it across. Now, you can confidently flip the cake onto a plate, remove the parchment paper, and let it cool completely.

To make the icing, while the cake is cooling, mix the powdered sugar and lemon juice in a small bowl until completely smooth. Then, using a teaspoon, decoratively drizzle the icing over the cake.

> **NOTES**
>
> *You can substitute sorghum flour with other gluten-free options like quinoa, millet, or oat flour.*

RHUBARB AND ORANGE BLOSSOM SCONES

MAKES 6 SCONES • V

There is so much that I love about scones! Whenever I journey to Scotland to spend time with family, I make a point of exploring charming Scottish cafes to indulge in a steaming pot of tea along with scones adorned with clotted cream and jam.

In this recipe, I've created a distinctive pastry by combining some familiar Iranian flavors with a classic Scottish scone.

3 cups (370 g) whole wheat pastry flour

½ cup (100 g) unrefined sugar

1 tablespoon baking powder

¼ teaspoon sea salt

½ cup (115 g) unsalted butter, chilled and cut into ¼-inch (6-mm) cubes

½ cup (60 g) diced rhubarb

⅔ cup (160 ml) whole milk, plus more as needed

1 tablespoon orange blossom water

Combine the flour, sugar, baking powder, and salt in a large mixing bowl. Add the chilled butter and use your fingertips to mix it to avoid excessively warming the butter. Keep doing this until the mixture looks like fine bread crumbs.

Add the rhubarb to the flour mixture and mix until coated. Then, combine the milk and orange blossom water and slowly pour it into the flour mixture while gently mixing with a fork. Continue mixing until a soft dough forms. Gather the dough into a ball without kneading it. If the dough feels too dry, add a small amount of milk to bring it together. Cover and place in the fridge to chill for 15 minutes.

Place the chilled dough on a lightly floured work surface. Flatten it with your hands to create a rectangle that is about 1½ inches (4 cm) thick. Cut out the dough using a 2½-inch (6-cm) circular cutter and place on a baking sheet lined with parchment paper. Reshape the leftover dough and continue cutting until all of the dough is used up. You should get about six scones.

Place the baking sheet in the fridge for another 10 minutes while you preheat the oven to 350°F (180°C).

CONTINUED

Place the scones in the oven and start baking. You'll know they're done when they've risen a bit and hold their shape and the bottom is lightly browned, about 20 minutes. Remove the scones from the oven and cool on a wire rack.

Scones are best when they are still warm, topped with a dollop of clotted cream or butter and jam, and accompanied by a cup of tea.

> **NOTES**
>
> *Traditionally, scones are made with all-purpose or cake flour for a light and fluffy texture. However, I prefer to use whole-grain pastry flour, sacrificing a bit of lightness for a more flavorful and nutritious scone.*
>
> *Start with cold butter and mix the dough gently without overworking it. Chilling the scones in the fridge before baking keeps the butter cold and helps them rise better, making them lighter.*
>
> *For added color, you can brush the scones with milk, melted butter, or beaten egg before baking.*

Bastani Sonati

SAFFRON ICE CREAM

MAKES 1½ QUARTS (1.4 L); 10 SERVINGS • V GF

Bastani sonati is an ice cream that's familiar and deeply endearing to all Iranians. For me, it conjures up images of hot summer days growing up in Tehran and on the shores of the Caspian Sea. After a long day of swimming and building sandcastles at the beach, I often finished the day's activities with ice cream.

- 2 cups (480 ml) heavy cream, divided
- 3 cups (720 ml) whole milk, divided
- 3 tablespoons arrowroot powder
- 1 cup (200 g) unrefined sugar
- ½ teaspoon mastic powder (optional)
- ⅛ teaspoon sea salt
- ½ teaspoon vanilla extract
- ½ teaspoon saffron threads, ground using a smooth mortar and pestle
- 2 tablespoons rose water
- 2 tablespoons raw pistachios, coarsely chopped

First, let's prepare the frozen cream base. Pour ½ cup (120 ml) of the heavy cream onto a small flat plate and pop it in the freezer for about an hour until it's frozen solid.

In a small mixing bowl, combine ⅓ cup (80 ml) of the milk with the arrowroot and stir until it's completely smooth. Set it aside for now.

Combine the remaining 1½ cups (360 ml) of heavy cream, remaining 2⅔ cups (640 ml) of milk, sugar, mastic powder (if using), salt, and vanilla in a large saucepan. Bring it to a gentle simmer over medium-high heat and simmer for about 10 minutes, stirring frequently to prevent any milk from crusting on the bottom.

When the milk starts to steam (but well before it comes to a boil), reduce the heat to low. Add the saffron and rose water to the saucepan and stir. The mixture should become vibrantly golden and quite aromatic.

Give the arrowroot and milk mixture one more stir and add it to the saucepan. Raise the heat to medium and continue to stir until the mixture has thickened slightly, about 5 minutes.

CONTINUED

Remove from the heat, transfer to a shallow bowl, and allow the mixture to cool, about 20 minutes. Cover and refrigerate it for at least 2 hours (or overnight).

It's time to churn our ice cream. Transfer the chilled milk mixture to an ice cream maker and process it according to the manufacturer's instructions. This usually takes less than 30 minutes.

Take the previously frozen heavy cream out of the freezer and break it into roughly ½-inch (12-mm) pieces. Add them and the pistachios to the final stage of the ice cream maker's churning process. The ice cream will have a soft and creamy texture at this stage and is ready to be served. Alternatively, it can be returned to the freezer for 1 hour for a firmer texture.

> **NOTES**
>
> *Mastic is a resin that elevates both sweet and savory dishes, providing a subtle, distinctive flavor and a slight chewy texture. It definitely contributes something unique, but because bastani sonati contains many other fragrant ingredients, you can skip the mastic if you find it hard to obtain.*
>
> *Bastani sonati is often nestled between two thin wafers and served as a sandwich. Of course, it can also simply be scooped into a serving dish and served as is.*

Keyk Yazdi

CARDAMOM AND ROSE WATER CUPCAKES

MAKES 12 CUPCAKES • V

Keyk yazdi—named after the ancient city of Yazd—is to Iranians as chocolate cupcakes are to many Americans. For anyone with Iranian roots, this familiar treat stirs up sweet and tender emotions, often leading to nostalgic tales of enjoying keyk yazdi in Iran.

- 2½ cups (310 g) whole wheat pastry flour
- 2 teaspoons ground cardamom
- 2 teaspoons baking powder
- ¼ teaspoon baking soda
- ¼ teaspoon salt
- ½ cup (115 g) unsalted butter, gently melted
- 1 cup (200 g) unrefined cane sugar
- 2 large eggs
- 1 cup (240 ml) plain whole milk yogurt
- ¼ cup (60 ml) rose water
- 1 tablespoon pistachios, finely chopped

Preheat the oven to 350°F (180°C).

To prepare your muffin tins, lightly grease them with an oil spray or use cupcake liners.

In a large mixing bowl, combine the flour, cardamom, baking powder, baking soda, and salt and mix well.

In a separate large bowl, combine the butter and sugar, whisking them together until thoroughly incorporated. Add the eggs, yogurt, and rose water, whisking until you have a creamy consistency.

Gradually add the dry ingredients to the wet ingredients, gently folding everything together using a spatula until just combined, taking care not to overmix the batter.

Fill the muffin tins with the batter and sprinkle the pistachios on top. Place the cupcakes in the oven and bake for 20–25 minutes. You'll know they're ready when they turn golden brown, cracks form on top of the cupcakes, and a toothpick inserted into a center comes out clean.

Take the cupcakes out of the oven and transfer them to a serving platter. To keep your cupcakes fresh, store them in an airtight container for up to five days.

Ferni

SILKY ROSE RICE PUDDING

MAKES 8 SERVINGS · V GF

For me, ferni embodies the universal themes of love and attentiveness in the kitchen, delivering comforting, delicious food to your family.

It seems that I'm not alone. When I published this recipe on my blog, a culinary student from long ago responded to say how much she loved "to stand at the stove stirring the pudding and zoning out while listening to music." She continued, "And the end result was worth all the work . . . sweet and silky with that perfect hint of rose. It was pure comfort food, and I can't wait to make it again."

4 cups (960 ml) whole milk, cold, divided

½ cup (80 g) white rice flour

½ cup (100 g) unrefined cane sugar, or to taste

3 tablespoons rose water

2 tablespoons pistachios, finely chopped

NOTES

While the ingredients list and assembly process are straightforward, this pudding demands patience and dedication to continuous tending and stirring.

Combine 1 cup (240 ml) of the milk with the rice flour in a mixing bowl and whisk to blend. Set it aside to rest for 30 minutes.

Place the remaining 3 cups (720 ml) of milk in a saucepan and put it on the stove over medium heat. Allow the milk to come to a gentle simmer, 5–7 minutes.

Now, it's time to stir and add the flour and milk slurry you prepared earlier. Whisk continuously to ensure that no lumps form during this step. Once all of the flour mixture has been fully incorporated, stir in the sugar.

Reduce the heat to low, switch to a flat wooden spatula, and continuously stir the pudding for another 20 minutes, ensuring nothing sticks to the pan's bottom.

Add the rose water and stir for another 5 minutes. The pudding should have a custard consistency that will further thicken as it cools. Be sure to taste the pudding and check that the flour is silky smooth and doesn't feel gritty under your teeth.

Remove the saucepan from the heat. Use a ladle to divide the pudding among eight individual serving bowls, about ½ cup (120 ml) each.

Ferni can be served warm or chilled. If serving chilled, place it uncovered in the fridge for 2 hours. Garnish with the pistachios before serving.

CHAPTER 10

BEVERAGES

Yogurt and Mint Soda • **V GF**
Dugh • 220

Sweet and Sour Mint Cordial • **VG GF**
Sharbat Sekanjebin • 222

Iranian-Inspired Minty Gin and Tonic • **VG GF**
Sekanjebin Cocktail • 223

Citrusy Chia and Rose Water Cordial • **VG GF**
Tokhm Sharbati • 225

Rose and Cantaloupe Drink • **VG GF**
Pāludeh • 226

Boulder Chai • **VG GF**
227

V • VEGETARIAN   **VG** • VEGAN   **GF** • GLUTEN FREE

THE WEIGHT OF HOPE

MILNATHORT, SCOTLAND, AND SEATTLE, WA | 2022

In 2022, life for many of us seemed to be reverting to its usual course as the world gradually recovered from the Covid pandemic. My days were occupied with familiar routines: attending to my therapy clients; passionately teaching Iranian cuisine; developing recipes, writing, and taking photos for my blog; and relishing once again the joys of traveling.

I was also relishing the sense of belonging that came from having emotionally reconnected with Iran and being deeply involved in my community. At the same time, I had opened myself up to the feelings associated with distance, sadness, and longing for Iran. If I wanted to stay connected with Iran, I needed to hold space for all of the emotions that it evoked.

I married into a Scottish family, and the quaint town of Milnathort in Scotland holds warm memories for me. Nevertheless, it's also now sadly associated with feelings of grief and pain. In September 2022, while visiting Milnathort for a happy family event, I first learned of the arrest and tragic killing of Mahsa Jina Amini, a young Kurdish woman, in the custody of the so-called morality police in Tehran. The news sent a shockwave through my heart, magnifying my consciousness of the contrast between the privileges we mostly enjoy in the Western world and the oppression and limitations on one's autonomy in Iran. The feeling of duality is hard to put into words. My awareness of the two worlds—one in upheaval, the other seemingly unchanged—was a constant challenge.

Describing the next few months as tumultuous and heavy would be an understatement. It was disheartening that major news agencies provided scant coverage of the uprising that followed Mahsa's death. Iranians in the diaspora, of course, shared information fervently. My mornings began with a ritual of sifting through various news outlets and social media sources, seeking updates, and following various events and figures who played active roles, all before starting my day's work. At the end of each day, I threw myself more than ever before into preparing meals at home: Cooking became my primary coping mechanism.

What also helped was the network of connections that emerged between old and new friends. Amid our conversations, previously untold stories of grief, trauma, and the pain of disconnection were interwoven with glimmers of hope: dreams of change, reconnection, and *āzādi* (the Persian word for freedom).

Far from the streets of Tehran, and without any real influence on events as they developed, I nevertheless sought whatever agency I could find. In December, food once again became my form of activism. I organized two dinners, bringing together eighty attendees for a five-course Iranian meal while providing a platform for speakers to share information and raise awareness. To my classes I added context and explanation about the situation in Iran. Cooking at home had helped me cope; teaching and storytelling now gave me hope.

> **Hope is being able to see that there is light despite all of the darkness.**
>
> —ARCHBISHOP DESMOND TUTU

As 2022 came to a close and 2023 began, hopes for change persisted. However, the movement slowed and a sense of uncertainty crept in. When a force, a momentum, suddenly halts, you are left to evaluate the parts of your life put on hold, the toll on your mental and physical health, and the guilt of being able to move on. I gradually resumed my daily routine, distancing myself from the news from Iran, which, as the movement began to fade, felt like a painful reminder of defeat.

Yet hope endures. Change takes time, and celebrating life and finding joy in the face of oppression can be an act of defiance in itself.

Thus, I resolved to embrace the joy that food brings to my life. I attended cooking classes and practiced in my own kitchen to deepen my understanding of other cuisines. I hosted intimate dinners to maintain my connection with my local community and organized more fundraising events. I finally started to write this book. I expanded my Iranian cooking classes, developing new courses that cover Iranian street food, stuffed dishes, and classic stews, all with the aim of sharing stories and raising awareness of this beautiful cuisine and rich culture that deserve celebration.

I have once again found a new balance on the hyphen that defines my life: being Iranian-American, belonging to both places, and yet not fully belonging to either.

Dugh

YOGURT AND MINT SODA

MAKES 4 SERVINGS • V GF

The unique combination of yogurt, carbonated water, and mint in dugh creates a tangy and fizzy taste that awakens the senses. What sets dugh apart from other drinks is the omission of sugar in favor of salt, creating a pleasing interplay between yogurt's tang, mint's freshness, and salt's savoriness.

- 2 cups (480 ml) whole milk European-style yogurt
- 2 cups (480 ml) sparkling water
- 1 teaspoon sea salt
- 2 teaspoons dried mint
- 4 sprigs fresh mint leaves
- ½ teaspoon ground rose petals

Combine the yogurt, sparkling water, salt, and dried mint in a bowl. Whisk gently until smooth, taking care not to overmix, as it may cause the sparkling water to lose its fizziness. To serve, place a handful of ice cubes into each serving glass and pour the dugh over them. Garnish with the fresh mint and rose petals.

NOTES

You can prepare dugh with either still water or a mix of sparkling and still water. For a lighter drink, consider using low-fat yogurt instead of full-fat.

Salt is an essential component of dugh, as it helps balance the yogurt's tartness, but feel free to adjust the amount to suit your preference.

Dugh complements kababs wonderfully, especially on a hot summer day.

Sharbat Sekanjebin

SWEET AND SOUR MINT CORDIAL

MAKES 8 SERVINGS • VG GF

Long before the rise of processed, sugary sodas, Iran had a variety of refreshing beverages called sharbat. These chilled drinks boast vibrant colors and enticing flavors, with three essential components: acidity, sweetness, and flavor.

This sharbat features a syrup known as sekanjebin, a combination of sugar, wine vinegar, and mint.

FOR THE SEKANJEBIN

1 cup (240 ml) water

1 cup (240 ml) white wine vinegar

2½ cups (500 g) unrefined sugar

1 cup (30 g) fresh mint

FOR THE SHARBAT

3 cups (720 ml) cold water

1 Persian cucumber, grated

1 lime, thinly sliced

½ cup (15 g) fresh mint

To make the sekanjebin, in a saucepan, combine the water, vinegar, and sugar. Stir and bring to a gentle boil over medium-high heat. Once little bubbles break through the surface, reduce the heat to medium and simmer for about 30 minutes. Turn off the heat, add the mint, and let the pan stand for at least 15 minutes to infuse the syrup with a deep, minty taste and aroma. Remove the mint using a slotted spoon and place the syrup in the fridge to cool.

When you're ready to make the sharbat, grab a pitcher, mix 1 cup (240 ml) of the sekanjebin with the cold water, and stir in the cucumber. To serve, place a handful of ice cubes in each serving glass and fill with sharbat. Garnish each glass with a slice of lime and a few mint leaves.

Sekanjebin can be prepared in advance and kept in the fridge for up to 2 weeks.

> **NOTES**
>
> *This recipe makes more sekanjebin syrup than you will need for the sharbat. You can use the surplus as a cocktail ingredient (see opposite). More traditionally, try dipping fresh lettuce leaves into a bowl of sekanjebin for a crispy, tangy, minty bite.*
>
> *Adjust the ratio of sekanjebin to water in the sharbat to deliver a more robust or milder flavor, according to your taste.*

Sekanjebin Cocktail

IRANIAN-INSPIRED MINTY GIN AND TONIC

MAKES 1 SERVING • VG GF

My favorite cocktail, particularly in summertime, is the gin and tonic, whether a classic version or one elevated with aromatics like cardamom or rhubarb. In this variation, I've added a uniquely Iranian touch by introducing sekanjebin, a mint and vinegar syrup. Unapologetically untraditional, this fusion of cultures and tastes makes this cocktail extra special.

2 oz (60 ml) gin

1 oz (30 ml) sekanjebin (opposite)

2 drops Angostura bitters

4–6 oz (120–180 ml) tonic water

1 sprig fresh mint

1 seedless green grape, thinly sliced

Start by filling a highball glass with ice cubes.

Pour your favorite gin over the ice, and then add the sekanjebin. Feel free to adjust the amount of syrup to your taste, depending on how sweet you want your cocktail.

Add the bitters to bring depth and complexity to the mix, and gently stir all of the ingredients.

To finish the cocktail, top off the glass with the tonic water. Give it a final stir, and garnish with the mint and grape slices.

Cheers! Or as we say in Persian, *beh salāmati*, meaning "to your health!"

Tokhm Sharbati

CITRUSY CHIA AND ROSE WATER CORDIAL

MAKES 4 SERVINGS • VG GF

Refreshing and unique, this beverage combines the flavors of rose and lime with the intriguing texture of swollen chia seeds.

- 3 cups (720 ml) water
- ⅓ cup (70 g) unrefined sugar
- 2 tablespoons chia seeds
- Juice of 3 limes
- ¼ cup (60 ml) rose water
- 1 lime, thinly sliced
- 4 fresh mint leaves

In a saucepan, combine the water and sugar, stir, and bring to a gentle simmer over medium heat to dissolve the sugar, about 5 minutes. Remove from the heat, add the chia seeds, lime juice, and rose water, give it a stir, and chill in the fridge for 1 hour.

To serve, fill glasses with ice cubes and pour the sharbat over them. For a final touch, garnish each glass with a slice of lime and a mint leaf before serving.

> **NOTES**
>
> In Iran, this sharbat is most commonly made with basil seeds, which you can find at Iranian stores or through online retailers. However, for this recipe I've used chia seeds, which are more readily available.
>
> Feel free to customize the sharbat to your liking by adjusting the quantities of the sweet and sour ingredients.

Pāludeh

ROSE AND CANTALOUPE DRINK

MAKES 6 SERVINGS • VG GF

This is another of Iranian cuisine's many flavorful beverage choices. Pāludeh takes ripe cantaloupe to new heights with rose water syrup and crushed ice, making it a perfect treat for hot summer days. (See photo on page 216.)

½ cup (120 ml) water

½ cup (100 g) unrefined cane sugar

2 tablespoons rose water

1 small cantaloupe (about 1½ lb/680 g), peeled, seeded, cut into quarters, and chilled

1 cup (150 g) crushed ice or ice cubes

Fresh mint leaves, for garnish

In a small saucepan, bring the water and sugar to a simmer over medium heat while stirring. Reduce the heat to low and simmer until the sugar has completely dissolved and the syrup has reduced slightly, 5–7 minutes.

Add the rose water, stir, and remove the saucepan from the heat. Transfer the syrup to a suitable jar and chill in the fridge for 1 hour.

Grate the cantaloupe into a large bowl. Add the rose syrup and ice to the grated cantaloupe and stir.

To serve, select four decorative glasses and fill each with the pāludeh mixture using a ladle. Garnish with fresh mint leaves for a final touch.

> **NOTES**
>
> *I often prepare extra rose syrup, storing it in my fridge for up to 2 weeks, which makes it easy to whip up pāludeh. Additionally, I enjoy drizzling it over fresh fruit, pancakes, and even using it in cocktails.*
>
> *You can substitute 2 tablespoons of rose water mixed with 4 tablespoons (80 g) of honey for the ½ cup (120 ml) of rose syrup used in this recipe.*
>
> *While I like the texture of grated cantaloupe, you can easily blend it in a high-speed blender for a smoother consistency.*

BOULDER CHAI

MAKES 4 SERVINGS • VG GF

After I graduated from culinary school in Boulder, I had the opportunity to return as a teacher. I had crafted a curriculum for vegan baking, which it was my privilege to teach for many years.

As I prepared to teach my first class, I wondered how I could best integrate myself into the kitchen amid all the ongoing training.

Offering guests a cup of tea is a cherished tradition in Iran, so I decided to welcome the students with steaming cups of soy chai. An extra-special touch was using freshly prepared soy milk from the prior tofu-making class.

My Boulder chai was a signature that became synonymous with my classes at the school.

- 3 cups (720 ml) water
- 2-inch (5-cm) cinnamon stick
- 10 green cardamom pods
- 4 whole cloves
- 1 star anise pod
- ½ teaspoon fennel seeds
- ½ teaspoon black peppercorns
- ½-inch (12-mm) piece of fresh ginger, sliced
- 3 tablespoons loose-leaf or 4 tea bags black tea
- 3 cups (720 ml) unsweetened soy milk
- ⅓ cup (80 ml) maple syrup, or to taste

Begin by bringing the water to a boil in a saucepan over high heat.

Using a mortar and pestle, crush the spices into small pieces. Add the spices to the boiling water, reduce the heat to low, and simmer for 5 minutes. Add the tea and let it steep for 2 minutes before adding the soy milk and maple syrup. Increase the heat to high and bring the tea mixture to a gentle boil before removing it from the heat. Pour through a fine-mesh strainer, and serve hot.

NOTES

Experiment by adjusting the spice quantities, dry-roasting the spices, or steeping them longer in water. You can also use different types of tea, such as rooibos or green tea, and different plant-based milks, such as oat, almond, or coconut. Sweeten your chai with honey or unrefined cane sugar, or omit the sweetness entirely.

EPILOGUE

AMERICAN CUISINE

When you think about it, it's extraordinary that this child from the shores of the Caspian Sea has made his home on the shores of the Salish Sea. Named for the Indigenous Coast Salish People, the Salish Sea includes Puget Sound, where Seattle is located, specifically on the ancestral land of the Duwamish, Suquamish, Stillaguamish, and Muckleshoot People. I could not finish this book without a heartfelt acknowledgment of the culinary opportunities that my adopted country has given me.

In every nation in the world, no matter how distinctive its cuisine, every region and probably every family has its own recipes and food traditions. This may be even more the case in the United States than anywhere else, given its blending of cultures. So to the question "What is American cuisine?" there are many equally valid answers. My own view is undoubtedly influenced by my very specific experience: as an immigrant, as a resident of certain regions of the country, and through my exploration of some—but by no means all—of the global food traditions found in America.

To me, American cuisine represents an exquisite blend of cultural influences, starting with the ancestral foods and rich traditions of the Indigenous Peoples of this land. Layered onto this foundation are the contributions of the immigrants who, for many and complex reasons, have found a home here. The United States is often referred to as a melting pot, and that is perhaps represented most clearly in the range of foods found here. Dishes considered authentic or traditional in their places of origin have been combined and adapted, shaped by the land's capacity to cultivate essential ingredients. For example, many Southern dishes such as gumbo are believed to derive from Native American, West African, and European traditions combined. And when I prepare my Iranian favorites, I often substitute hard-to-acquire ingredients out of sheer necessity. Many herbs that grow abundantly in the Caspian Sea region simply aren't cultivated in North America and can't be imported due to sanctions on Iranian exports.

In my own household, we enjoy hamburgers and pizza, tofu and tempeh, tacos and chile relleno, soba and udon noodles—the list goes on. All of these serve as reminders of what America has come to mean to me: a place where cultures come together. America has given me the opportunity to explore and embrace many diverse culinary traditions. Though I don't have direct familial ties to these cultures, I've cultivated a deep affinity and appreciation for Japanese, Korean, Vietnamese, Thai, Indian, Mexican, and Navajo cuisines, all of which I first encountered in the United States.

My kitchen is stocked with an extensive range of ingredients, representing diverse global food traditions that reach far beyond Iranian cuisine. Creating my own tofu, tempeh, miso, and kimchi feels as natural and dear to me as preparing a hearty Iranian stew. In the end, I'm not defined by a single cuisine; instead, I'm shaped by the love and dedication poured into food preparation and the exploration of culinary traditions, regardless of their origin.

In America, individuals like me find the freedom to celebrate a wide range of tastes and traditions.

BUTTERNUT SQUASH MACARONI AND CHEESE

MAKES 6 SERVINGS • V

I asked friends from Seattle to Switzerland to name the quintessential American dish, and the clear favorite was mac and cheese. Because I first tasted it within a few days of my arrival in the United States, that truly resonated with me.

For me, mac and cheese is as emblematic of American tradition as a classic apple pie, bringing me the same sense of comfort as a platter of delicate and fluffy Iranian rice. It also offers endless possibilities for adaptation and elevation.

To me, this embodies the essence of America, a place that afforded me the freedom and opportunity to define my identity and embrace a diverse world of flavors.

FOR THE BUTTERNUT SQUASH

1 butternut squash (2½–3 lb/1.1–1.4 kg)

1 tablespoon olive oil

½ teaspoon sea salt

1 cup (240 ml) whole milk

FOR THE TOPPING

2 tablespoons olive oil

1 large shallot, minced

2 cloves garlic, minced

½ teaspoon paprika

4 fresh sage leaves, finely chopped

¼ teaspoon sea salt

1 cup (100 g) panko bread crumbs

Begin by preheating the oven to 400°F (200°C).

To prepare the butternut squash, cut the squash in half using a sharp, sturdy knife. Remove the seeds from the center with a spoon. Rub the cut sides of the squash with the oil, sprinkle them with the salt, and place both halves face down on a baking sheet.

Put the baking sheet into the preheated oven. The roasting time can vary depending on the squash's size, typically up to 45 minutes. To check for doneness, insert a fork; the flesh should be completely soft.

Once the butternut squash is fully roasted, take it out of the oven. Use a spoon to scoop the squash out from the skin. You'll need about 2 cups (280 g) of cooked squash (you can freeze the rest for future use). Place the squash in a high-speed blender, add the milk, and blend until you have a smooth and creamy sauce-like consistency. Set aside.

Reduce the oven temperature to 350°F (180°C).

FOR THE PASTA

4 quarts (3.8 l) water

2 tablespoons sea salt

1 lb (450 g) cavatappi or other short cut pasta

FOR THE SAUCE

¼ cup (60 g) unsalted butter

¼ cup (30 g) all-purpose flour

2 cups (480 ml) whole milk

1 teaspoon sea salt

¼ teaspoon chipotle pepper powder

4 oz (115 g) extra-sharp white Cheddar cheese, grated

2 oz (60 g) Gruyère cheese, grated

½ cup (60 g) freshly grated Parmesan cheese

NOTES

You can prepare the butternut squash in advance to save time.

To make the topping, heat a frying pan over medium-low heat, add the oil, and sauté the shallot until it's lightly browned and aromatic, 3–4 minutes. Add the garlic and sauté for another couple of minutes, then add the paprika, sage, and salt. Stir and add the panko bread crumbs. Continue stirring for 2 minutes, then remove from the heat and set aside.

To prepare the pasta, bring the water and salt to a boil in a large stockpot and cook the pasta until it's just shy of al dente, 6–8 minutes. Make sure that the pasta isn't fully cooked, as it will continue to cook later in the oven. Strain and rinse with cool water, then set aside.

To make the sauce, melt the butter in a saucepan over medium-low heat and add the flour. Whisk until the butter and flour are fully integrated and lightly aromatic, about 2 minutes. Slowly add the milk while whisking to avoid any lumps.

Raise the heat to medium and whisk until the sauce begins to thicken, 8–10 minutes. Add the salt, chipotle pepper, and puréed squash to the sauce, stirring to integrate fully. Finally, add all of the cheeses and keep stirring until they're melted, creating a beautiful golden orange sauce.

In a large bowl, combine the pasta with the sauce, mixing well. Transfer the mixture to a 9 by 13-inch (23 by 33-cm) baking dish. Evenly spread the topping over the pasta and bake until golden brown and bubbly, about 20 minutes. Remove it from the oven and allow it to rest for a few minutes before serving.

ACKNOWLEDGMENTS

This book would not have been possible without the love and support I've received from these wonderful human beings:

My mother, not only for nurture and sustenance during my childhood but also for invaluable insights and guidance on the traditions and techniques of preparing Iranian cuisine.

Julianaa Satie, who's had an extraordinary influence on my life, both teaching me about food and helping me discover my soul and purpose.

Peter Behravesh, my editor, who believed in me, steadfastly supported my vision for this book, and patiently guided me through the maze of the publishing world as my advocate.

Wendy Sherman, who was prepared to represent me as a first-time author, despite her impressive existing clientele. When I needed support, she was my dedicated champion.

Marjan Kamali, whose inspiring writing influenced a key theme of this book, and whose introductions within the publishing world helped bring it to fruition. Her wisdom, friendship, and support during particularly difficult times have left a lasting and profound impression.

Paola Albanesi, **Leila Nabizadeh**, **Nasrin Noori**, **Zahra Razeghi**, **Sahar Shomali**, and **Nadia Tommalieh**, who generously shared their knowledge and soulful recipes with me.

Lynann Bradbury, **Ariana Bundy**, **Naz Deravian**, **Cathia Geller**, **Betsy Jones**, **Kevin Jones**, **Janet Kimball**, **Cynthia Lair**, **Eleni Ledesma**, **David Paynter**, **Anne Phillips**, **Eric Rose**, **Robin Westby**, and **Misha Zadeh**, who contributed their own unique insights and wisdom, generously dedicating their time to our engaging conversations about the book, greatly enhancing its content.

Brandi Henderson and all my colleagues at The Pantry, who provided me with a platform in the community kitchen to share my stories, teach my craft, and build a community through the art of Iranian cuisine.

Pat Benatar, whose music has been a constant and inspiring soundtrack throughout my life, spanning forty years of concerts, backstage meet-ups, and dancing in my kitchen.

ABOUT THE AUTHOR

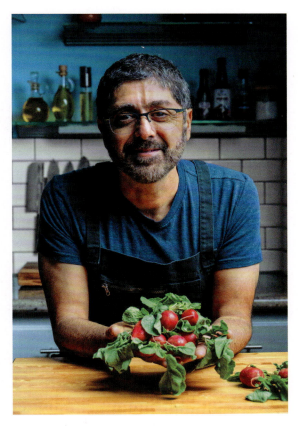

Photograph by Sama K. Rahbar

Omid Roustaei is an Iranian-American chef and culinary instructor who has been deeply involved in the culinary world for more than twenty years. Born and raised in Tehran, he attended the School of Natural Cookery in Boulder, Colorado, where he studied the art of intuitive cooking.

Omid now balances a career as a psychotherapist with his enthusiasm for teaching and writing. He shares Iranian culture and traditions through cooking and storytelling, using the power of food to foster connections and serve as a gentle form of advocacy and activism. His writing can be found at thecaspianchef.com, and he is a regular contributor to The Kitchn and The Spruce Eats. This is his first cookbook.

INDEX

A
āb ghureh (verjuice or verjus)
  about, 16
  bean soup with herbs and noodles, 50, 51–52
  eggplant with herbs and poached eggs, 154, 155
  minty cucumber and tomato salad, 30
Afghan mushroom curry, 80, 81
Afghan rice pilaf with lamb, 114, 115–16
almonds
  Afghan rice pilaf with lamb, 114, 115–16
  sour cherry rice with petite meatballs, 97–98, 99
apple and parsnip soup, creamy, 53
Arab bread, 192–93
āsh, about, 42

B
baguette, crispy, feta pesto on a, 32, 33
barberries
  about, 16
  fresh herb kuku, 60, 61
  saffron barberry rice with braised chicken, 109–10, 111
  stuffed fish with herbs and barberries, 179–81, 180
barley soup with beans and herbs, 48–49
beans
  barley soup with beans and herbs, 48–49
  bean soup with herbs and noodles, 50, 51–52
  beef and herb stew, 133–34, 135
  cilantro rice with chickpeas, 112–13
  falafel kuku, 64
  fava beans with poached eggs and crispy shallots, 138, 139–40
  green bean rice with beef, 103–4, 105
  kale and crispy chickpea salad, 31
beef
  beef and herb stew, 133–34, 135
  beef and herb stew with rhubarb, 136–37
  beef and yellow split pea stew with crispy potatoes, 156–58, 157
  beef stew with poached eggs, 142, 143–44
  fried potato and bulgur kibbeh, 34, 35–36
  green bean rice with beef, 103–4, 105
  petite meatballs with crispy potatoes, 151–52, 153
  sour cherry rice with petite meatballs, 97–98, 99
beets
  beet salad with tarragon dressing, 27
  citrus and beet salad with fennel dressing, 24, 25–26
beverages
  Boulder chai, 227
  citrusy chia and rose water cordial, 224, 225
  Iranian-inspired minty gin and tonic, 223
  rose and cantaloupe drink, 226
  sweet and sour mint cordial, 222
  yogurt and mint soda, 220, 221
Boulder, CO, 90–91
Boulder chai, 227
breads
  Arab bread, 192–93
  feta pesto on a crispy baguette, 32, 33
  Iranian flatbread, 189–91, 190
  Iranian sourdough flatbread baked on hot pebbles, 194–96, 197
  savory cheese pastries, 186, 187–88
bulgur and fried potato kibbeh, 34, 35–36
burdock, braised, with carrots, 78, 79
burger, tempeh, with mango salsa, 168–70, 169

C
cakes
  cardamom and rose water cupcakes, 212, 213
  saffron and lemon olive oil cake, 204–6, 205
cantaloupe and rose drink, 226
cardamom and rose water cupcakes, 212, 213
carrots
  Afghan rice pilaf with lamb, 114, 115–16
  braised burdock with carrots, 78, 79
  creamy smoked fish and vegetable soup, 46–47, 47
  roasted carrots with feta sumac spread, 82, 83
  saffron carrot halva, 202, 203
  saffron carrot rice with braised tofu, 100, 101–2
cauliflower steaks with creamy tomato sauce, 86–87
chai, Boulder, 227
cheese
  butternut squash macaroni and cheese, 228, 232–33
  feta pesto on a crispy baguette, 32, 33
  pomegranate and cucumber salad, 28, 29
  roasted carrots with feta sumac spread, 82, 83
  saffron risotto, 122–23
  savory cheese pastries, 186, 187–88
chia and rose water cordial, citrusy, 224, 225
chicken
  chicken in pomegranate and walnut sauce, 130, 131–32
  chicken in tangy walnut and herb sauce, 159–60
  chicken stew with roasted peppers and prunes, 145–46, 147
  grilled saffron chicken kababs, 171–73, 172
  peach and saffron chicken stew, 148, 149–50
  saffron barberry rice with braised chicken, 109–10, 111
chickpeas
  barley soup with beans and herbs, 48–49
  bean soup with herbs and noodles, 50, 51–52
  cilantro rice with chickpeas, 112–13
  falafel kuku, 64
  kale and crispy chickpea salad, 31
chimichurri tahini sauce, grilled corn with, 72, 73
chives
  feta pesto on a crispy baguette, 32, 33
  salmon with za'atar and herb sauce, 177
  walnut kuku, 65
cilantro
  barley soup with beans and herbs, 48–49
  bean soup with herbs and noodles, 50, 51–52
  beef and herb stew, 133–34, 135
  broiled halibut with tamarind and herb sauce, 178
  chicken in tangy walnut and herb sauce, 159–60
  cilantro rice with chickpeas, 112–13
  falafel kuku, 64
  feta pesto on a crispy baguette, 32, 33
  fresh herb kuku, 60, 61
  fresh herb rice with fish, 119–21, 120
  grilled corn with tahini chimichurri sauce, 72, 73
  potato and herb egg drop soup, 44, 45
  spiced herb rice with prawns, 117–18

stuffed fish with herbs and
   barberries, 179-81, *180*
citrus and beet salad with fennel
   dressing, *24*, 25-26
citrusy chia and rose water cordial,
   224, 225
corn, grilled, with tahini chimichurri
   sauce, 72, *73*
cucumbers
   citrus and beet salad with fennel
      dressing, *24*, 25-26
   feta pesto on a crispy baguette,
      32, *33*
   lettuce cups with cucumbers and
      yogurt sumac dressing, 22, *23*
   minty cucumber and tomato
      salad, 30
   pomegranate and cucumber
      salad, *28*, 29
   roasted sunchokes with cucumber
      yogurt spread, 84, *85*
   sweet and sour mint cordial, 222
cupcakes, cardamom and rose
   water, 212, *213*
curry, Afghan mushroom, 80, *81*

D
dashi, vegan, 74
desserts
   cardamom and rose water
      cupcakes, 212, *213*
   rhubarb and orange blossom
      scones, 207-8
   saffron and lemon olive oil cake,
      204-6, *205*
   saffron carrot halva, *202*, 203
   saffron ice cream, 209-11, *210*
   silky rose rice pudding, 214-15
dill
   barley soup with beans and
      herbs, 48-49
   bean soup with herbs and noodles,
      50, 51-52
   feta pesto on a crispy baguette,
      32, *33*
   fresh herb kuku, 60, *61*
   fresh herb rice with fish, 119-21, *120*
   potato and herb egg drop soup,
      44, 45
   salmon with za'atar and herb
      sauce, 177
   spiced herb rice with prawns, 117-18
   walnut kuku, 65

E
eggplant
   braised Japanese eggplant, 74-75
   eggplant and tomato stew with
      sour grapes, 161-63, *162*
   eggplant kuku, 66, *67*
   eggplant with herbs and poached
      eggs, *154*, 155
eggs. *See also* kukus
   beef stew with poached eggs,
      142, 143-44

butternut squash rice with
   sunny-side-up eggs, *106*, 107-8
eggplant with herbs and poached
   eggs, *154*, 155
fava beans with poached eggs and
   crispy shallots, *138*, 139-40
fenugreek soup with poached eggs,
   54, 55
potato and herb egg drop soup,
   44, 45
spinach and herbs with poached
   eggs, 141

F
falafel kuku, 64
fennel
   citrus and beet salad with fennel
      dressing, *24*, 25-26
   kale and crispy chickpea salad, 31
fenugreek
   about, 16
   fenugreek soup with poached eggs,
      54, 55
fish
   broiled halibut with tamarind and
      herb sauce, 178
   creamy smoked fish and vegetable
      soup, 46-47, *47*
   fresh herb rice with fish, 119-21, *120*
   salmon with za'atar and herb
      sauce, 177
   stuffed fish with herbs and
      barberries, 179-81, *180*
fruit. *See specific fruits*

G
garlic, fried, 42
gin and tonic, Iranian-inspired
   minty, 223
golpar (Persian hogweed), about, 16
grapes, sour, eggplant and tomato
   stew with, 161-63, *162*
green bean rice with beef, 103-4, *105*

H
halibut, broiled, with tamarind and
   herb sauce, 178
halvah, saffron carrot, *202*, 203
herbs. *See also specific herbs*
   dried, soaking, 129
   fresh, preparing, 129
   in Iranian cuisine, 129

I
ice cream, saffron, 209-11, *210*
ingredients, 16-17
Iranian flatbread, 189-91, *190*
Iranian-inspired minty gin and
   tonic, 223
Iranian sourdough flatbread baked
   on hot pebbles, 194-96, *197*

K
kababs
   grilled lamb kababs, 174-76, *175*

grilled saffron chicken kababs,
   171-73, *172*
kale and crispy chickpea salad, 31
kashk (fermented whey)
   about, 16
   barley soup with beans and herbs,
      48-49
   bean soup with herbs and noodles,
      50, 51-52
   butternut squash spread with whey
      and mint, 76-77
   drizzling over soup, 42
khoresh, about, 128-29
kibbeh, fried potato and bulgur, *34*,
   35-36
kombu
   vegan dashi, 74
kukus
   about, 59
   eggplant kuku, 66, *67*
   falafel kuku, 64
   fresh herb kuku, 60, *61*
   potato kuku, *62*, 63
   walnut kuku, 65

L
lamb
   Afghan rice pilaf with lamb, *114*, 115-16
   grilled lamb kababs, 174-76, *175*
lemon and saffron olive oil cake,
   204-6, *205*
lentils
   barley soup with beans and herbs,
      48-49
   bean soup with herbs and noodles,
      50, 51-52
lettuce
   chilled pea and lettuce soup, 43
   lettuce cups with cucumbers and
      yogurt sumac dressing, 22, *23*
lime
   citrusy chia and rose water cordial,
      224, 225
limu omāni (Persian dried limes)
   about, 16-17
   beef and herb stew, 133-34, *135*
   beef and yellow split pea stew with
      crispy potatoes, 156-58, *157*

M
macaroni and cheese, butternut
   squash, *228*, 232-33
mango salsa, *169*, 170
meat. *See* beef; lamb
meatballs
   petite meatballs with crispy
      potatoes, 151-52, *153*
   sour cherry rice with petite
      meatballs, 97-98, *99*
Milnathort, Scotland, 218-19
mint
   beef and herb stew with rhubarb,
      136-37
   butternut squash spread with whey
      and mint, 76-77

237

chicken in tangy walnut and herb sauce, 159–60
eggplant with herbs and poached eggs, *154*, 155
fried mint, 42
Iranian-inspired minty gin and tonic, 223
minty cucumber and tomato salad, 30
pomegranate and cucumber salad, *28*, 29
spinach and herbs with poached eggs, 141
stuffed fish with herbs and barberries, 179–81, *180*
sweet and sour mint cordial, 222
walnut kuku, 65
yogurt and mint soda, 220, *221*
mushrooms
    Afghan mushroom curry, 80, *81*
    vegan dashi, 74

N

nira (garlic chives)
    fresh herb kuku, 60, *61*
    fresh herb rice with fish, 119–21, *120*
noodles and herbs, bean soup with, *50*, 51–52
nuts. *See specific nuts*

O

olives
    chicken stew with roasted peppers and prunes, 145–46, *147*
    kale and crispy chickpea salad, 31
onion, fried, 42
orange blossom water
    about, 17
    rhubarb and orange blossom scones, 207–8
oranges
    citrus and beet salad with fennel dressing, *24*, 25–26
    saffron carrot rice with braised tofu, *100*, 101–2

P

parsley
    barley soup with beans and herbs, 48–49
    bean soup with herbs and noodles, *50*, 51–52
    beef and herb stew, 133–34, *135*
    beef and herb stew with rhubarb, 136–37
    chicken in tangy walnut and herb sauce, 159–60
    eggplant with herbs and poached eggs, *154*, 155
    falafel kuku, 64
    feta pesto on a crispy baguette, *32*, 33
    fresh herb kuku, 60, *61*
    fresh herb rice with fish, 119–21, *120*
    grilled corn with tahini chimichurri sauce, *72*, 73
    potato and herb egg drop soup, *44*, 45
    salmon with za'atar and herb sauce, 177
    spinach and herbs with poached eggs, 141
    stuffed fish with herbs and barberries, 179–81, *180*
    walnut kuku, 65
parsnip and apple soup, creamy, 53
pasta and noodles
    bean soup with herbs and noodles, *50*, 51–52
    butternut squash macaroni and cheese, *228*, 232–33
pastries, savory cheese, *186*, 187–88
pea and lettuce soup, chilled, 43
peach and saffron chicken stew, *148*, 149–50
peppers
    chicken stew with roasted peppers and prunes, 145–46, *147*
    kale and crispy chickpea salad, 31
    mango salsa, *169*, 170
pesto, feta, on a crispy baguette, *32*, 33
pistachios
    Afghan rice pilaf with lamb, *114*, 115–16
    cardamom and rose water cupcakes, 212, *213*
    saffron barberry rice with braised chicken, 109–10, *111*
    saffron carrot halva, *202*, 203
    saffron carrot rice with braised tofu, *100*, 101–2
    saffron ice cream, 209–11, *210*
    silky rose rice pudding, 214–15
    sour cherry rice with petite meatballs, 97–98, *99*
pomegranate and cucumber salad, *28*, 29
pomegranate molasses
    about, 17
    chicken in pomegranate and walnut sauce, *130*, 131–32
potatoes
    beef and yellow split pea stew with crispy potatoes, 156–58, *157*
    beef stew with poached eggs, *142*, 143–44
    creamy smoked fish and vegetable soup, 46–47, *47*
    fenugreek soup with poached eggs, *54*, 55
    fried potato and bulgur kibbeh, *34*, 35–36
    green bean rice with beef, 103–4, *105*
    petite meatballs with crispy potatoes, 151–52, *153*
    potato and herb egg drop soup, *44*, 45
    potato kuku, *62*, 63
    walnut kuku, 65
poultry. *See* chicken
prawns, spiced herb rice with, 117–18
prunes and roasted peppers, chicken stew with, 145–46, *147*
pudding, silky rose rice, 214–15

R

radishes
    feta pesto on a crispy baguette, *32*, 33
    lettuce cups with cucumbers and yogurt sumac dressing, 22, *23*
raisins
    Afghan rice pilaf with lamb, *114*, 115–16
rhubarb
    beef and herb stew with rhubarb, 136–37
    rhubarb and orange blossom scones, 207–8
rice
    Afghan rice pilaf with lamb, *114*, 115–16
    barley soup with beans and herbs, 48–49
    butternut squash rice with sunny-side-up eggs, *106*, 107–8
    cilantro rice with chickpeas, 112–13
    cooking tips, 93
    fresh herb rice with fish, 119–21, *120*
    green bean rice with beef, 103–4, *105*
    in Iranian cuisine, 92–93
    rice with a crispy saffron layer, *94*, 95–96
    saffron barberry rice with braised chicken, 109–10, *111*
    saffron carrot rice with braised tofu, *100*, 101–2
    saffron risotto, 122–23
    silky rose rice pudding, 214–15
    sour cherry rice with petite meatballs, 97–98, *99*
    spiced herb rice with prawns, 117–18
risotto, saffron, 122–23
rose water
    about, 17
    cardamom and rose water cupcakes, 212, *213*
    citrusy chia and rose water cordial, *224*, 225
    rose and cantaloupe drink, 226
    saffron carrot halva, *202*, 203
    silky rose rice pudding, 214–15

S

saffron
    about, 17
    chicken in pomegranate and walnut sauce, *130*, 131–32
    fresh herb rice with fish, 119–21, *120*
    grilled saffron chicken kabobs, 171–73, *172*

238

peach and saffron chicken stew, *148*, 149–50
rice with a crispy saffron layer, *94*, 95–96
saffron and lemon olive oil cake, 204–6, *205*
saffron barberry rice with braised chicken, 109–10, *111*
saffron carrot halva, *202*, 203
saffron carrot rice with braised tofu, *100*, 101–2
saffron ice cream, 209–11, *210*
saffron risotto, 122–23
sour cherry rice with petite meatballs, 97–98, *99*
salads
  beet salad with tarragon dressing, 27
  citrus and beet salad with fennel dressing, *24*, 25–26
  kale and crispy chickpea salad, 31
  lettuce cups with cucumbers and yogurt sumac dressing, *22*, *23*
  minty cucumber and tomato salad, 30
  pomegranate and cucumber salad, *28*, 29
salmon with za'atar and herb sauce, 177
salsa, mango, *169*, 170
San Jose, CA, 184–85
scones, rhubarb and orange blossom, 207–8
Seattle, WA
  An American Identity, 70–71
  The Caspian Chef, 200–201
  Embracing the Apron, 126–27
  Reconnection, 184–85
  The Therapist Within, 166–67
  The Weight of Hope, 218–19
Sedona, AZ, 58–59
shallots, crispy, and poached eggs, fava beans with, *138*, 139–40
shellfish. *See* prawns
soda, yogurt and mint, 220, *221*
soups
  āsh, about, 42
  barley soup with beans and herbs, 48–49
  bean soup with herbs and noodles, *50*, 51–52
  chilled pea and lettuce soup, 43
  creamy parsnip and apple soup, 53
  creamy smoked fish and vegetable soup, 46–47, *47*
  fenugreek soup with poached eggs, *54*, 55
  potato and herb egg drop soup, *44*, 45
  toppings for, 42
sour cherry rice with petite meatballs, 97–98, *99*
spinach
  barley soup with beans and herbs, 48–49

bean soup with herbs and noodles, *50*, 51–52
potato and herb egg drop soup, *44*, 45
spinach and herbs with poached eggs, 141
squash
  butternut squash macaroni and cheese, *228*, 232–33
  butternut squash rice with sunny-side-up eggs, *106*, 107–8
  butternut squash spread with whey and mint, 76–77
stews
  about, 128–29
  beef and herb stew, 133–34, *135*
  beef and herb stew with rhubarb, 136–37
  beef and yellow split pea stew with crispy potatoes, 156–58, *157*
  beef stew with poached eggs, *142*, 143–44
  chicken in pomegranate and walnut sauce, *130*, 131–32
  chicken in tangy walnut and herb sauce, 159–60
  chicken stew with roasted peppers and prunes, 145–46, *147*
  eggplant and tomato stew with sour grapes, 161–63, *162*
  eggplant with herbs and poached eggs, *154*, 155
  fava beans with poached eggs and crispy shallots, *138*, 139–40
  peach and saffron chicken stew, *148*, 149–50
  petite meatballs with crispy potatoes, 151–52, *153*
  spinach and herbs with poached eggs, 141
sumac
  about, 17
  fried potato and bulgur kibbeh, *34*, 35–36
  lettuce cups with cucumbers and yogurt sumac dressing, *22*, *23*
  roasted carrots with feta sumac spread, *82*, 83
sunchokes, roasted, with cucumber yogurt spread, *84*, 85
sweet and sour mint cordial, 222
Swiss chard
  kale and crispy chickpea salad, 31

T
tahdig, about, 92–93
tahini
  falafel kuku, 64
  grilled corn with tahini chimichurri sauce, 72, *73*
tamarind
  about, 17
  broiled halibut with tamarind and herb sauce, 178

tarragon
  beet salad with tarragon dressing, 27
  chilled pea and lettuce soup, 43
tea. *See* chai
Tehran, Iran, 40–41
Tehran and Daryakenar, Iran, 20–21
tempeh burger with mango salsa, 168–70, *169*
tofu, braised, saffron carrot rice with, *100*, 101–2
tomatoes
  Afghan mushroom curry, 80, *81*
  beef stew with poached eggs, *142*, 143–44
  cauliflower steaks with creamy tomato sauce, 86–87
  citrus and beet salad with fennel dressing, *24*, 25–26
  eggplant and tomato stew with sour grapes, 161–63, *162*
  eggplant with herbs and poached eggs, *154*, 155
  fenugreek soup with poached eggs, *54*, 55
  minty cucumber and tomato salad, 30
  petite meatballs with crispy potatoes, 151–52, *153*

V
vegetables. *See specific* vegetables

W
walnuts
  butternut squash spread with whey and mint, 76–77
  chicken in pomegranate and walnut sauce, *130*, 131–32
  chicken in tangy walnut and herb sauce, 159–60
  feta pesto on a crispy baguette, *32*, 33
  fresh herb kuku, 60, *61*
  lettuce cups with cucumbers and yogurt sumac dressing, *22*, *23*
  stuffed fish with herbs and barberries, 179–81, *180*
  walnut kuku, 65

Y
yellow split pea and beef stew with crispy potatoes, 156–58, *157*
yogurt
  lettuce cups with cucumbers and yogurt sumac dressing, *22*, *23*
  roasted carrots with feta sumac spread, *82*, 83
  roasted sunchokes with cucumber yogurt spread, *84*, 85
  yogurt and mint soda, 220, *221*

Z
za'atar and herb sauce, salmon with, 177

weldonowen
an imprint of Insight Editions
P.O. Box 3088
San Rafael, CA 94912
www.weldonowen.com

CEO Raoul Goff
VP Publisher Roger Shaw
Publishing Director Katie Killebrew
Editor Peter Adrian Behravesh
Assistant Editor Amanda Nelson
VP, Creative Director Chrissy Kwasnik
Art Director & Designer Megan Sinead Bingham
Production Designer Jean Hwang
Sr Production Manager Joshua Smith
Sr Production Manager, Subsidiary Rights Lina s Palma-Temena

Photography by Waterbury Publications, Inc.
Author photograph on page 235 and back cover © Sama K. Rahbar

Weldon Owen would also like to thank Catherine Alioto, Karen Levy, Mary Cassells, and Elizabeth Parson for their work on this book.

Text © 2025 Omid Roustaei
Foreword © 2025 Lauren Ko

All rights reserved. No part of this book may be reproduced in any form without written permission from the publisher.

ISBN: 979-8-88674-183-4

Manufactured in China by Insight Editions
10 9 8 7 6 5 4 3 2 1

Insight Editions, in association with Roots of Peace, will plant two trees for each tree used in the manufacturing of this book. Roots of Peace is an internationally renowned humanitarian organization dedicated to eradicating land mines worldwide and converting war-torn lands into productive farms and wildlife habitats. Roots of Peace will plant two million fruit and nut trees in Afghanistan and provide farmers there with the skills and support necessary for sustainable land use.